Preaching that *Connects*

a method
for developing
preaching that is in tune
with the hearers, planned
jointly and carefully
balanced.

Howard D. Vanderwell

WIPF & STOCK · Eugene, Oregon

Wipf and Stock Publishers
199 W 8th Ave, Suite 3
Eugene, OR 97401

Preaching That Connects
A Method for Developing Preaching That is in Tune
With the Hearers, Planned Jointly and Carefully Balanced
By Vanderwell, Howard D.
Copyright©1989 by Vanderwell, Howard D.
ISBN 13: 978-1-5326-6362-8
Publication date 7/24/2018
Previously published by R. C. Law & Co., Inc., 1989

CONTENTS

CHAPTER ONE

What Makes The Difference?

We stand by the oceanside on a sunny afternoon and watch the kite-flyers practice their skills. The delightful breeze that sweeps off the waters lifts the colorful crafts while their masters carefully direct them by pulling on the strings first one way and then another. Our heads turn upward to watch their movements and our spirits seem to soar as the kites float on one delightful breeze after another.

We marvel at such skilled flyers. They seem to know exactly how to capture the breezes for maximum effect; they are able to control the movements of the craft precisely, and they know just what must be done to bring the kite safely back to earth again.

I wonder, while I watch, about all those efforts I had made to fly kites in my day. The breezes seemed different then, more fickle, more unpredictable. I tried to put the kite up high and orchestrate some attractive swoops in the sky, but the only thing that happened can best be described as one determined attempt on the part of the kite to divebomb and crash onto the beach. Then I wondered just what it is that makes one kite fly so gracefully, and another swoop down in a crash. What is it that makes the difference?

Sermons are like kites, and so are preachers! Some soar so

gracefully, swept up by the gentle breezes of the Spirit, lifting all heads and spirits up to the sky. Others wobble around and then without warning crash back to earth. Some preachers seem able to take advantage of those spiritual currents; while others are victims of competing currents. Some preachers are masters who lift our spirits; others leave those spirits restlessly on the beach.

We all, of course, want our sermons to cause spirits to soar, but it's a sad fact that not all do. Why? What makes the difference?

NO SIMPLE TASK

If flying a kite well is no simple task, surely preaching is not! There are lots of pressures and competing winds present when the preacher mounts the pulpit on Sunday morning. There are the pressures of competing interests in the hearts and minds of the worshipers who fill the pews. Even before they came, they felt it. It would have been appealing to stay under the covers, or go out for a round of golf instead. The adolescent in the family possibly raised his weekly protest about going to church — again! Even after they are present the pressure of distractions is within each worshiper. The young man finds it intensely difficult to concentrate on the sermon when last night's date is uppermost in his mind. The young mother, weary after a demanding week of family responsibilities, would rather slump in the pew than soar in the spirit. The business man finds it easier to go over the details of the proposal he must present at the office tomorrow than the preacher's line of thought. One candid worshiper told me he has designed more homes during my sermons than he cares to admit. Another claims his mind busily arranges for the sale of his lot full of cars. Will these preaching events really make any difference at all?

There is also pressure within the preacher. It really starts in earnest early Sunday morning, though he feels its rumblings already Saturday evening. A huge but invisible question mark seems to descend from the sky and wrap itself around him in a deadly strangle-hold. As it pulls tighter he feels it wring those weekly questions out of his heart again: "Who am I to be standing here before these people in worship?

How will I ever be able to cause their spirit to soar? What if my 'kite' crashes on the beach this morning? If only I had another day or two to prepare!"

Actually that kind of pressure has been there all week. He has come to expect it as an integral part of his ministry. Sunday always seems to loom up more rapidly than it should.

THE DIFFERENCE

What makes the difference between whether the kite soars or crashes? What makes the difference between whether the sermon lifts spirits or leaves them restless on the beaches of life? Though many factors influence it, one consideration is primary: the success or failure of a sermon will in large part be determined by whether it makes direct connection with the world of the worshiper. A kite may be precisely built and beautifully colored, but if it fails to connect with blowing breezes it will go nowhere. So it is with a sermon. It may be meticulously organized with highly descriptive terms, impressive vocabulary, and correct exegesis, but if it fails to connect with winds in the life of the worshiper nothing will happen.

The thesis of this book, therefore, is that the preacher needs to be realistically in tune with the circumstances and needs of his hearers. True, his interpretation of the Word of God must be accurate and faithful, and his thoughts must be presented logically and clearly, with words that are appropriately chosen. But even the most carefully designed sermon will fail if it has not taken into careful consideration the events and experiences of the hearers.

Suppose you are a troubled citizen of a southern racially torn town. Tension between the blacks and whites in your neighborhood is running high. Bloody confrontations took place in the city park yesterday and it's obvious that's not the end of the matter. Confused and disturbed you enter church on Sunday morning and discover that the message is called "The LOGOS Concept in the Gospel of John". This learned discussion of a theological concept may be very impressive in a classroom somewhere, but your spirit, so badly in need of some encouragement, gets none.

Or suppose that the week has been a frightening one for you because you have learned that your wife has been unfaithful. You have been shocked to discover that she has been carrying on a sinful relationship with one of your friends for several months. When you confronted her on Thursday evening she packed her bags and left. Your whole world has come crashing down and now lies at your feet like so much broken glass. With a broken spirit you creep into the worship service Sunday morning only to be confronted by an extended pulpit discussion of whether the rapture will be pre- or post-tribulational. You couldn't care less about such an issue! Your heart longs for some breeze, but gets none.

Now, imagine a situation where the news has stunned your community that five high-school students from your congregation were seriously injured in an automobile accident Wednesday evening on their way to a basketball game. It's uncertain at this point what the prognosis is for several of them. Your heart is heavy, concerned about their welfare, and feeling deeply for their parents and families. But this time the worship service is just what you need. The Pastor intercedes lovingly in prayer for the hurting ones, and his sermon focuses on the loving care that God provides for those who are victims of suffering and tragedy. The compassion of Christ is central and you leave with new breezes of the Spirit blowing strongly in your heart.

Or imagine that your Pastor received the grim news this week that he has cancer. A small lump was removed a week ago and he seemed confident that it was not a major problem. But now pathology reports a significant malignancy. The congregation is stunned. What will it mean? How serious is it? Can it be treated? How are the pastor and his wife handling it? Are they crushed? Can they cope with it? With such questions whirling in your mind you come to worship Sunday morning, and discover that the pastor does not evade the issue. He does not pretend that everything is fine. He admits his concerns and fears, but also expresses confidence and trust in the Lord. His message focuses on the promises of the Father's loving care for His children even in times of great stress when there is no way of knowing what the future will bring. He explains that the faith to which the Bible calls us does not demand that we have answers to all our questions. You go home from that service with the awareness that you have been face to face with reality and that the loving presence of God surrounded you. You have experienced the winds of the Spirit blowing in turbulent times.

Let's return to our original inquiry. What makes some kites soar and others dive? What causes some sermons to lift hearts and spirits while others only leave them restless on the ground? The difference is found in how effectively the sermon connects with the real world of the worshiper's experiences. You can't expect a sermon that is not deliberately crafted to make that connection to communicate well. To be sure, the Holy Spirit takes your words and uses them however he desires to touch hearts and lives. However, the Spirit's work is no substitute for carefully crafted sermons aimed to meet the worshiper's world. The development of such a craft, therefore, is essential.

COMMUNICATION IS COMPLEX

The preacher who is able to carefully develop the craft of writing such sermons will understand and accept the complexity of the process of verbal communication.

Eugene Nida says we must always remember that communication involves three essential factors: the sender of the message, the message to be sent, and the receptor of the message. To neglect any one of the three will abort good communication, but a neglect of the receptor seems most common. He warns: "...people tend to overlook the importance of the receptor, for they assume that in communication the only important elements are the source and the message...however, the way in which the receptor 'decodes' the message has as much effect upon its meaning as the way in which the source 'encodes' it." [1] So the relationship between the sender and the receptor is a very delicate and complicated one that greatly influences the accuracy of the message.

When a sender aims to communicate a message, he must "encode," or formulate and package, it in a way that he believes is appropriate to the given situation. This is often so automatic that we are not conscious of doing so. Our thoughts must be formulated into words, our words must be structured into sentences, and our sentences must be surrounded with mannerisms. Therefore, as we speak, we reflect our attitude toward the subject and the receptor, and reveal our emotional state at the time of speaking along with our purposes in communicating. On the basis of such considerations we will select words, adapt them, structure thoughts, and carry with them such gestures, mannerisms, style, type of voice, etc. as we consider appropriate. We must make these decisions and selections on the basis of our knowledge of the audience. Though often done automatically and unconsciously, we must see this as an important part of the communication process.

Our aim as those who send the message is to pave the way for those who receive the message, to enable him to "decode" it as accurately as possible. Nida says,

> ...the decoder's mind is not like a telephone exchange, in which an incoming call can be automatically switched to the proper circuit. Rather, our minds are like some of the huge so-called 'thinking machines,' though almost infinitely more complex; and any impulse, in the form of a word or sentence, must not only be decoded in terms of its linguistic forms but must also filter through the grid of our own background experience if we are to have corresponding conceptions.[2]

It becomes clear, then, that a speaker or writer must know his audience. He must know their background, orientation, attitudes, readiness, etc. growing out of present and past experiences. Such knowledge will enable him to make wise choices in formulating (encoding) his message in such a way that will do justice to both the content of the message and the conditioning of the hearers.

For that reason, the discipline of Rhetoric and Public Speaking has always included audience analysis as one of its concerns. Anyone studying public speaking is told effectiveness is impossible without it.

Most major textbooks on public speaking emphasize it.

Unfortunately, not much attention is given to that in preaching. "Let the preacher prepare himself," he is told. "Prepare your message carefully," others say. But few are saying, "Study your hearers carefully."

ANOTHER STEP

We must, therefore, insert another step in the process of preparing to preach. In addition to the preparation of the preacher and the preparation of the message, an analysis of the congregation is demanded.

But now we have given the preacher a much larger responsibility. It makes preaching more difficult than before. Now that he must be aware of the worshiper's experiences, he must not only study the Word of God, but also carefully study the world of the worshiper. It calls him to the task of "dual exegesis". He must engage in faithful biblical exegesis so that his message is faithful to God's intent, and he must also engage in a careful exegesis of the world of human events so that he is able to speak to the needs of his hearers.

The preacher has, in all likelihood, learned exegetical skills during his training for the ministry. Now, he must learn the skill of the exegesis of human experience. But seminary classrooms don't teach that; he must learn that while he serves.

It isn't so hard to learn to exegete the experiences of ten or twenty worshipers in a small congregation whose experiences are similar to his. However, it becomes very difficult when there are hundreds of worshipers, many of whom live in a world that is quite different from his. How does he keep in touch with all their concerns and needs when they are so diverse? How can he know what they experience and what their care demands? Exegeting Scripture is difficult enough. Do we not make his task virtually impossible when we add this responsibility?

While it's true that this makes his task much more difficult, difficulty is never a legitimate reason for discarding a responsibility. The preacher must live with this conviction — that effective preaching will take place best when he connects with the world of the worshipers' experiences. Since that is true he must choose between less work and less effectiveness or more work and more effectiveness. The choice should not be difficult if he is properly committed to his task and calling, but carrying out that choice will be difficult!

Preachers must learn to consciously read and study about life in general, but also live among their parishioners to come to know their joys, cries and questions. When they do, they will receive hundreds and thousands of impressions each month that they must process and assimilate in order to draw certain reliable conclusions about their hearers. They must develop and use certain tools that will assist them to do this, and include a number of forums where the insights of others can be received.

No preacher should ever be intimidated into remodeling truth to fit the preferences or desires of his hearers. Consequently, the final decisions in the preaching process belong to the preacher, but he must always aim to communicate that truth in a way that connects with the worshiper's world he has come to know.

A realization of the difficulty of this task can be the preacher's ally to drive him to seek the assistance that he needs to do the task well. Without significant assistance this task cannot be done, but with the proper assistance it can be done — and well.

HELP FROM WHERE?

Of course, even to suggest to some preachers that they need assistance in their weekly task sounds very threatening. "I am accountable only to God. He has called me to this prophetic office and has equipped me to carry it out. No one else is in a position to tell me what to preach or how to do it. The prophetic office stands alone! The Spirit will lead me!" You can imagine a preacher rising to such a defense.

He is certainly correct to insist that he is ultimately accountable to God for the final choices of what he preaches and the truth he conveys. But we ought to realize that many preachers, and even lay leaders in the church, are far too willing to accept a couple of critical fallacies. One fallacy is that preachers are capable and reliable enough to be entrusted with the entire process of planning. Another is that the process of planning to preach is simple enough for one person to do it. Either way, the result is the same — sermon planning becomes a lonely task conducted in solo fashion. The preacher does it all alone, and that's terribly risky!

How can one preacher be sure that he understands the diversity of needs and concerns present in his congregation? How can one preacher be sure to hear all the cries for help? Or that he interprets them accurately? Which preacher would dare to claim he is free from prejudices and hobbies? Which preacher would dare to claim that he has no blind spots?

Therefore, I am proposing that, to overcome these risks, we call in two assistants.

1. **Lay leaders.** There is no substitute for the valuable insight a preacher gains from lay leaders. Nearly all congregations include lay leaders of some sort who supervise the spiritual life of the congregation. Some call them Elders, or Presbyters, or Deacons, or Trustees, or give them some other title. These lay leaders live and walk in the world of the other parishioners all week and are able to give valuable assistance to the preacher in understanding the world of his hearers. However, the church has never carefully developed its understanding of the task of such lay leaders. Most fail to see their office and task in this light and have deserted the preacher when he has needed them the most. It will be necessary therefore to examine the Biblical description of the office of lay spiritual leader in order that those in such a role may broaden their sense of responsibility.

2. **Advanced Planning.** Surveys indicate that most preachers plan a few months ahead at the most. Many, however, live week to week with no more advanced planning than that. Little material has been written and published about methods of advanced planning in preaching. Too little planning means running great risks. Creative messages that communicate concisely require incubation periods. The

more advanced planning a preacher does, the greater is the possibility that his messages will creatively break through the facade and communicate directly to his hearers. So it is necessary for us to set forth a method for planning an entire year's preaching.

There is nothing very satisfying seeing a preacher's kite smash to the ground time after time. Pastor, your sermons must fly! By considering what follows in this book, your preaching can be vastly different, so different that most of your sermons will fly. That difference is urgently needed.

1. Eugene A. Nida, *Message and Mission* (So. Pasadena, CA: Wm. Carey Library, 1972), p. 33, 34.

2. Ibid., p. 69, 70.

CHAPTER TWO

Situational Preaching

Since understanding the audience is such a crucial part of good public communication, preachers ought to be intolerant of preaching that fails to be sensitive to the situation of the hearers. Yet such insensitivity abounds.

Charles Spurgeon once warned students: "I know a minister who is great upon the ten toes of the beast, the four faces of the cherubim, the mystical meaning of the badger's skins, and the typical bearing of the staves of the ark, and the windows of Solomon's Temple; but the sins of businessmen, the temptations of the times, and the needs of the age, he scarcely ever touches upon."[1]

Another tells of the time when a group of engineers was assigned to a deserted post in Egypt. They eagerly anticipated the day when the preacher would pay them a visit and feed their hungry souls, but their anticipation turned to disappointment when the message he presented to them concentrated on the need to observe the Saint's Days on the religious calendar![2]

John Stott has generalized such a complaint when he said, "The characteristic fault of evangelicals is to be biblical but not contemporary, and the characteristic fault of liberals is to be contemporary but not biblical."[3]

SOME RESISTANCE

Many of us who stand in the pulpit will deny the legitimacy of such complaints. We'll also resist the charge that we have to do more analysis before we preach.

Can't you hear us? "I just don't think that's part of my work. For some guest speakers who are strangers, yes, but not for those of us who preach to the same congregation week after week. I just can't see why I must spend a lot of time and effort studying my congregation. After all, God took all their needs into consideration when he wrote the Bible, and as long as I preach the Bible I'm confident that their needs are going to be met. Besides, I have a special ally in the Holy Spirit who not only leads me in preaching but also is applying the Word to their hearts and lives. It's better that I spend my time studying the Bible, not people!"

What must I say to him? Does he have a point in claiming that the principles of audience analysis are not transferable to the local congregation? Is it true that the assistance of the Holy Spirit in applying the Word makes such a concern irrelevant for the preacher?

Some have tried to make that case. Indeed, probably far too many preachers have unconsciously taken this position and invested little effort into getting into the experiences of their listeners. D. Martyn Lloyd-Jones defends that position when he says in *Preaching And Preachers* that it is not necessary for the preacher to know the specific problems and sins of the people. There are, he says, "...general common needs...It is a vital point of preaching to reduce all listeners to that common denominator."[4]

He draws a contrast between the preacher and the physician. The physician, in order to treat a patient, must inquire into all the special and specific symptoms of the patient. The preacher does not need such detailed information, but needs only to be concerned about general symptoms.

However, in making such a claim, Lloyd-Jones seems to be concerned about those who might say that the preacher has to work in the factory for six months to preach to the factory worker, or become a drunk for six months to reach the drunkards, or attempt to enter all the professions of his parishioners before he can expect to reach them effectively. His additional concern is that emphasis on analyzing the audience will too easily create a situation where the pew will control the pulpit, and the pew will acquire a veto power over what the pulpit might address. We might all agree with him in both of those concerns.

But Lloyd-Jones, himself, is an illustration of the importance of analysis for effective preaching. In the introduction to his *Sermon On The Mount* he explains that "...if I had been left to my own choice I would not have chosen to preach a series of sermons on the Sermon on the Mount...(but) the particular reason for doing so is the peculiar condition of the life of the Christian Church..."[5] Again, he points to the same cause in the introduction to *Spiritual Depression Its Causes and Cures* when he says the need for these messages "...arose as the result of pastoral experience."[6] We should, therefore, learn balance from the reflections of Lloyd-Jones. Preaching must address the concerns and needs of the hearers, but the preacher must never allow the conditions of the hearers to override his own responsibility to be biblical.

DIVERSITY IN THE LOCAL CHURCH

But when the preacher starts looking at his congregation he will find a lot of diversity. Phillips Brooks presents a very balanced understanding of the situation when he speaks, on the one hand, of the constant and unchanging needs of men, and, on the other, of the ever-varying aspects of those needs. The message and its tone, therefore, must correspond with both the unchangeableness of some needs and the ever-varying aspects of others. Brooks insists that a knowledge of the unchanging needs of men comes from our study of the Word of God, but our knowledge of the ever-varying needs comes only through a diligent effort to watch events and people.[7]

The preacher who is in tune with his congregation looks out over his Sunday morning audience and sees much more than faces. He recognizes new parents who rejoice at the birth of their first child but are anxious about taking up the new responsibilities of parenthood, a widower who no longer finds any purpose for living since the death of his wife, a successful businessman who is pressured to cut corners ethically at the office and struggles with his Christian commitment, a new Christian struggling to cast off his former lifestyle, a skeptic whose heart will not let him abandon the Christian faith yet finds it so difficult to heartily embrace it, a sensitive young couple looking for some indication of God's call to special service and an angry, depressed mother.

Edgar N. Jackson expressed the diversity of the local congregation very strikingly.

> On the basis of compilation of averages it may be possible to get some concept of a cross section of your congregation. In a congregation of 500 people, it is responsible to assume that at least one hundred have been so recently bereaved as to feel an acute sense of loss. Probably a third of the married persons are facing problems of personality adjustment that may weaken or destroy their home life. At least half of the 500 can be assumed to have problems of emotional adjustment to school, work, home, or community that endanger their happiness. Others may have neuroses ranging from alcohol addiction to lesser forms of obsession and anxiety states. Perhaps 15 or more are homosexually inclined and another 25 depressed. Another 100 may be suffering from so great a feeling of guilt or fear of discovery that their peace of mind and health are jeopardized....[8]

That picture of a typical Sunday morning audience is not a bright one, and not the picture of health that most preachers would like to imagine. But it so graphically portrays the diversity of need that we ought never to enter our pulpit without a humble sense of mission.

Walter R. Bowie exhorted preachers to spend some time in the church on Saturday evening, walking from one pew to another, perhaps kneeling at each one, remembering those who will sit there tomorrow morning with all their varied needs. "Here they are, these different personalities with their different joys and sorrows, their opportunities and their needs. What can the message he plans to preach on Sunday be made to mean to them?"[9]

So the preacher who aims to communicate effectively must never be far from the experiences of his congregation. "It remains an axiom of Christian preaching that the road from the study to the pulpit runs through a living, demanding, interrupting manse, out into the noisy street, in and out of houses and hospitals, farms and factories, buses, trains, cinemas...up between rows of puzzled people to the place where you are called to preach...For the living Word there is no by-pass from study to pulpit."[10]

The preacher must build bridges of communication and aim to span the gulf between the Word and the world of the hearers. He must be equally familiar with both. A careful study of the New Testament will show that Christ and the Apostles each followed this method. Their addresses and their epistles reveal sensitivity to the needs and the situation of those they addressed. We will have an opportunity to examine that later.

LIFE-SITUATION PREACHING

Such considerations led to the development of what has been called "Life-situation preaching". It was largely an American development, aided by Higher Criticism, the development of pastoral psychology, and complaints against irrelevant preaching. The focus was placed on preaching that addressed man as he encountered life. Harry Emerson Fosdick has often been seen as it's major exponent, though many others such as Walter Russell Bowie, Arthur J. Gossip and Norman Vincent Peale are also noted for their contributions.

Fosdick pleaded for preaching that started with the problems of the people. If it did not, then it was a lecture, not a sermon. "Each sermon," he said, "should have for its main business the head-on constructive meeting of some problem which was puzzling minds, burdening consciences, distracting lives, and no sermon which so met a real human difficulty, with light to throw on it and help to win a victory over it, could possibly be futile."[11] He was willing to call preaching personal counseling on a group scale, but others went even farther and called it pulpit counseling, mass counseling, therapeutic preaching, problem-solving preaching, etc.

There are a number of concerns that we should have about this approach to preaching. Exponents of life-situation preaching have often held a low view of the authority of Scripture. Consequently, it has been easy for them to focus more on people and their problems than on God and his claim on our lives, to become moralistic and give more consideration to psychology than to the gospel, and to be preoccupied with the issues of time rather than the issues of eternity. Life-situation preaching can also lead to a lack of variety, dealing only with problems and problem-solving, while ignoring the grand sweep of redemptive events in the plan of God for the ages.

Yet we must not be too quick to dismiss life-situation preaching. If irrelevance is a problem in modern preaching, then greater attention to the "situation" of the listeners is the *sin qua non* of its improvement. A century ago Emerson spoke about "writing that is bloodwarm." Good preaching must be like that. Situational preaching, therefore, is needed. It must be preaching that is marked by a clear understanding of the Truth of God in the Scriptures, but must also be marked by a clear understanding of where people are living. Preaching that is sensitive to located difficulties in the lives of the listeners will avoid vague generalities and will provide a human screen through which the preacher must pass the material before it is preached.

One Sunday I attended the worship service of a large independent congregation in southern California. It has several thousand members, three Sunday morning services, a beautiful campus of classrooms, and a staff of eleven. The Senior Pastor presented a sermon that morning from Romans 15:1-13 entitled "Looking Out For One Another". It was obvious throughout that sermon that the preacher had read the situation of his congregation well. For the first ten minutes of the message he spoke of his concern for their "situation". They had grown rapidly as a congregation and were in the process of uniting members from different backgrounds, cultures, and life-styles. Such a situation, he warned, could easily lead to conflict, criticism, division and weakness within the congregational life. It was obvious, therefore, that he was intent on addressing the problem of diversity. His message focused on the early New Testament Church, their diversity within

Jewish/Greek/Roman culture and the potential divisiveness that existed there. Paul, he said, taught them the solution and the Holy Spirit wrote it down in Romans 15 for all churches in similar situations through the ages. It is acceptable, according to Paul, to have differences of conviction and opinion on matters that the Scriptures do not directly address. God calls his people to "Look Out For One Another" in brotherly love that resolves never to cause someone else to stumble. His sermon was an excellent example of Situational Preaching.

In my own experience, an event stands out in which I was jerked out of what might have been very irrelevant preaching. I had spent the morning working on a sermon concerning Labor Day for the coming Sunday. I was attempting to put together an outline, based on Genesis 1-3, that communicated the truths that our work should have dignity because it is essential to our humanness and includes us as partners with God in the management of creation. I planned also to point to Genesis 3:16-19 and indicate that our work today can expect to show the effects of sabotage because of the fall into sin. However, I had not planned to make a big point of that because I thought it sufficient merely to say, "I don't have to remind any of you of that because you experience it every day." Reasonably satisfied with the outline, I began to put the papers into the folder and return them to the drawer when there was a knock on the study door. A lady of the congregation asked if she could make a prayer request for Sunday. There were tears in her eyes as she spoke. "Pray for people who are experiencing so much stress on their jobs when policies and attitudes toward employees are changing so much," she pleaded. We chatted about it for a little while and she told me that her husband, an employee of some twenty years for the same company, had lost his interest and motivation in his work because the company had come under new management and pressure for greater productivity was intense. He even wondered how he could continue under such stress. She was burdened for him. As soon as she left, the file folder came out of my drawer again. I read over what I had written, and realized that it certainly was true but if I communicated it in that form it might well be perceived as true, but very idealistic and insensitive to the hurts and frustrations of those who, like her husband, are having trouble keeping their heads above water in the storms at work. I had exegeted the passage well, but her brief visit helped me exegete the life-situation so much better.

Good preaching comes from dual exegesis! Dual exegesis will overcome the preacher's cardinal sin — dullness. To avoid dullness you must not only catch the attention of the audience immediately but hold it throughout your presentation.

ADAPTATION

How can you be sure to do that? Only by adapting the presentation of your message to be in tune with their world. There are many factors involved but one of the greatest is your ability to talk their language, identify with their experiences, and understand their conscious and (as far as possible) unconscious motivations and needs. To put it into technical terminology, we are saying that your ability to encode the message in such a way that your hearers will be able to decode it easily and reliably will go a long ways to make your communication engaging, interesting and influential. Any speaker, therefore, must personally understand and appreciate the depth of what Atticus says in *To Kill A Mockingbird*: "You never really understand a person...until you climb into his skin and walk around in it."

A word of caution, however, is in order. When a speaker plans to adapt his presentation to effectively engage the audience's attention, God gives him no license to sacrifice principle or truth. His aim must not be that everyone in the audience likes him or is delighted with everything that he says. His sole aim in adapting his message is to make it clear. He wants his listeners to understand him, and he wants to hold their attention for a hearing of his message.

To be effective the disciplined preacher will adapt his sermon in several important ways. His adaptation will influence the **purpose** of his message. Obviously, a preacher should have a very different purpose in mind when he speaks to a group of parents celebrating the achievements of their children in an Honors Society Banquet, than he would when speaking to a group of parents who have formed a support group for parents of children with Leukemia. Similarly, he will have a different purpose when he speaks to a congregation expecting to celebrate Thanksgiving, than one which has gathered to mourn a community tragedy.

His adaptation will also affect his **selection of subject material.** When he leads worship at the community Rest Home he will deal with quite different material than when he speaks at a local Youth Rally. A congregation that has experienced the death of several younger members from cancer needs to hear different material than a congregation that is divided by racial unrest.

He must also pay attention to his **selection of rhetorical tools.** The words, structure of sentences, technical terminology, and also the manner in which the preacher presents himself must come under careful scrutiny. A congregation with a high level of education among its members will be able to handle tools that reflect refinement and precision. However, a rural congregation whose members have never gone past the eighth grade will need different tools.

The **organization** of the preachers message must also come under careful evaluation. When he preaches on a doctrinal issue over which there may be disagreements within the congregation, his organization must be precise, logical, with its claims well-substantiated. But when he is dealing with the subject of fears, for instance, his message may be built around pointed personal illustrations.

Finally, the **length of his message** must be considered. In some congregations a sermon of 20 minutes is considered appropriate; in others it would be an affront to conclude after such a short time.

My plea, then, is that the preacher must never enter the pulpit until he has carefully immersed himself in the life-situation of the hearers. Any sermon may be ever so nice when it lies on the desk, but the test of its real quality will come when the pastor enters the pulpit and the listeners sense whether or not he has lived in their world.

The faithful preacher is convicted that he must be God-centered in all he does, and Bible-centered in all he preaches. But if he is to communicate effectively he must also be audience-centered. If not, he runs the risk of writing and delivering an excellent sermon—for some other occasion or congregation. The preacher, immersed in the world of the Scriptures, will communicate the great truths of God only when he has also been immersed in the world of his hearers!

1. Charles H. Spurgeon, *Lectures,* First Series, p. 78, 79 in John R.W. Stott, *Between Two Worlds,* (Grand Rapids: Eerdmans, 1982), pp. 142, 143.

2. William M. MacGregor, *The Making of a Preacher,* (Philadelphia: Westminster, 1946), pp. 53, 54.

3. John R.W. Stott,The Demands of Biblical Exposition", an address at the Congress on Biblical Exposition, at Anaheim, California, March 5, 1986.

4. D. Martyn Lloyd-Jones, *Preaching And Preachers* (Grand Rapids: Zondervan, 1971), p. 134.

5. _____, *Sermon On The Mount* (Grand Rapids: Eerdman's, 1959), vol. I, p. 9.

6. _____, *Spiritual Depression; Its Causes and Cure* (Grand Rapids: Eerdman's, 1965), p. 5.

7. Phillips Brooks, *Lectures on Preaching* (Grand Rapids: Baker, n.d.), p. 219.

8. Edgar N. Jackson, *How To Preach To People's Needs* (Grand Rapids: Baker, 1956, pp. 14, 15.

9. Walter Russell Bowie, *Preaching* (New York; Abingdon, 1954), p. 28.

10. David H. C. Read, *The Communication The Gospel* (London: SCM Press, 1952), p. 47.

11. Harry E. Fosdick, *The Living of These Days,* (New York: Harper and Brothers, 1956). p. 94.

CHAPTER THREE

The Search
for Insight

This concept of dual exegesis that I advocate forms the preacher's approach to his task. He cannot expect to be effective unless he invests careful efforts into a double search. He searches the Word of God for the truth to communicate, and he searches the life of his congregation for insights that will help him communicate truth in a living, relevant way.

This is not an easy task. His schedule is already full. Demands on his time, attention and energy convince him that there are not enough hours in the day. Yet here is still another task. Is this inconsiderate? Is it asking for the impossible? No; there are no short-cuts to effectiveness. So the preacher must re-evaluate his method of study and his allocation of scheduled time; this task of studying his hearers cannot be ignored. He must **make** time for audience analysis.

OBSTACLES

Before turning our attention to the methods by which the preacher can analyze his congregation it is necessary to think about some obstacles that may stand in the way. There are significant obstacles to overcome. Some of them are so formidable that it will often be easy **not** to know your hearers well.

The size of the congregation is one of those obstacles. Studies show that the majority of congregations today have less than 275 worshipers at their Sunday morning services, but churches are growing larger. In a rural setting, with 150 homogeneous worshipers it is not difficult for the preacher to understand their needs accurately. But, in a suburban community where 500 or more worshipers gather on Sunday morning, the congregation will have lost much of its homogeneity and the preacher will find it much more difficult to get in touch with all their needs. Size, therefore, will often be a large obstacle.

Increased size and increased complexity usually go hand in hand. A small rural congregation will be less complex than a larger suburban or urban congregation. My first congregation of 55 families, 53 of whom were neighboring farmers, was relatively simple compared to the congregation of 250 families I now serve in which the whole range from farmers to retirees, blue-collar to professional people, singles to young families is represented. It follows, therefore, that the greater the complexity of the congregation, the greater the task of the preacher who aims to know them well. We may not hide from this reality, for American cities and villages are becoming less homogeneous and more complex. Communities no longer arise because of common pursuits and interests. Many communities are made up of people who commute to a wide variety of interests and vocations. Since the church is a reflection of the community in most areas, the preacher can expect more and more complexity within his congregation.

The tendency of preachers to move frequently is another major obstacle to knowing the congregation. The average length of pastorate varies a great deal from one family of churches to another, but statistics show that a typical pastorate may last anywhere from three to six years. That is too short a period in which to know the congregation intimately and build a ministry of preaching on the basis of that knowledge. It takes me between two and four years before I am confident that I have come to know and understand the general emotional, psychological and spiritual make-up of the congregation. By that time I have stored up enough experiences with them to understand their make-up and situation in life. Before that time I must rely on information and impressions received from others, only to discover that judgments and assessments made about their inner needs have to be corrected later on. A preacher, therefore, who moves to another congregation every five years forfeits the opportunity to increase his intimate knowledge of their needs and build his preaching ministry on it. This awareness led Phillips Brooks to point out that "...the long pastorates of other days were rich in the knowledge of human nature, in a very intimate relation with humanity." [1] And then he counsels preachers to, "First, have as few congregations as you can. Second, know your congregation as thoroughly as you can. Third, know your congregation so largely and deeply that in knowing it you shall know humanity."[2]

There is another insidious obstacle. All preachers face the fact that many people tend to put on a front in their presence. They behave artificially and conceal many of their real struggles and weaknesses. They want the preacher to think well of them instead of thinking realistically with them. Catherine Marshall tells that once her husband, Peter Marshall, told the men at Gettysburg Theological Seminary, "You must root your preaching in reality, remembering that the people before you have problems—doubts, fears, and anxieties gnawing at their faith. Your problem and mine is to get behind the conventional fronts that sit row upon row in pews..."[3] If we fail to overcome this obstacle we will never get accurate information about their needs.

The task to which we have set ourselves, therefore, has many pitfalls. It will take time, energy, and deliberate effort. The preacher who accomplishes this task well will have to draw on the efforts of others to assist him and will have to develop methods and tools to do so.

FOCUS OF ANALYSIS

In analyzing a congregation, the preacher should first note those matters that all members of all congregations have in common. From his convictions about man he will draw conclusions about the nature of people, that they are made in the image of God, that they are rational and moral beings, and that they possess a conscious self.

Beyond that he will look for those matters that **this** audience shares in common with one another, though not necessarily with other audiences. He will ask how **this group** is homogeneous. He will know that this is a congregation drawn together for worship because of their common beliefs and interests. But he must also note other common interests that may be present. Is this group reflective of a certain class of society in distinction from another group? Is there a common commitment to a certain viewpoint? Is there a history within this group that gives it a unique identity?

Then he will begin to focus on the variables. Is there a diversity here of age? Of sex? Of race? Of nationality? Of ethnic group? Do they represent many different walks of life? Must he assume similarity or dissimilarity in the group makeup?

The relation of the audience to the speaker is also significant. Is he a stranger or have they come to know each other well? Is he their pastor or a guest preacher? If he is their pastor, how long have they been together? Are they aware of his credentials and qualifications to speak to them or must he prove himself first? Do they respect and trust him or must he earn that? Are their convictions similar to or in conflict with his?

The relation of the audience to the occasion and the subject must also be considered. Are they a friendly audience who has come for inspiration, or an audience filled with skepticism? Are they a congregation that faithfully worships every week, a group that comes rather sporadically, or a group of students who are mandated to attend chapel? Do they have a high level of expectancy, or will they be content to pass the time? Have they made any preparations for their consideration of the subject, or must they first be drawn into the subject? Did they come to be entertained, inspired, informed, or persuaded?

In order to help speakers analyze audiences speech textbooks provide careful guidelines to apply. Preachers should not ignore these. Oliver, Cortright, and Hager, in *The New Training For Effective Speech,* suggest that every audience ought to be measured according to five categories: intelligence, interest, attitude, knowledge of the subject, and background.[4] Loren Reid, *First Principles of Public Speaking,* says, "You will need to answer questions like this:

1. What range of ages is present?
2. Are both sexes present?
3. What is the marital status of the listeners?
4. What trades, businesses or professions are represented?
5. What nationalities are represented?
6. What races are represented?
7. What religious faiths are represented?
8. What organizations are represented?
9. To what political parties do the listeners belong?
10. What is the educational background of the listeners?
11. Is the group essentially liberal or conservative?
12. What interests, needs, hopes, attitudes are represented?
13. What is the economic level of the group?

All of the above considerations are important, but there is another factor as well, a factor easily ignored because it is so intangible. I'm referring to the emotion of the audience: "The common denominator of every audience is their emotion. Love and grief and their opposites of hate and joy, with all their various gradations, run through every audience, no matter what the cultural status of the group."[6] Has this group gathered at a festive occasion with high spirits? Or is this a difficult situation to which they come depressed? Are they hostile or friendly, both to you and your subject material? Have they come to give thanks or to seek help? Lionel Crocker said,

> For the sake of convenience we may say that there are three types of emotions: (1) those which depress us and dissuade us from action, like sorrow, fear, shame, and humility; (2) those which elevate us and stimulate us to action, such as hope, patriotism, ambition, emulations, and anger; and (3) those which can both dissuade or persuade us—joy, love, esteem and pity.[7]

Obviously, therefore, the preacher must be in touch with the people of his audience.

METHODS OF ANALYSIS

It is time now to ask "how"? How can you learn the situations and the needs of the congregation to whom you preach? How can you gather reliable impressions? There are four methods that must be balanced against one another.

1. The preacher must **read.** The preacher will find that books and magazines are the gateway to the bigger world of humanity if he will only discipline himself to read more broadly than theological works. Every preacher feels the pressure of wanting to read more, yet having little time for it. There are no easy solutions to this problem, but the preacher who tires of the struggle, gives in to it, and fails to read is committing a grave error. Dr. Peter Eldersveld, well-known international radio minister on *The Back To God Hour* before his death in 1965, was recognized for understanding the spirit of his day exceptionally well. This enabled him to communicate with his radio listeners effectively. When asked what contributed to that awareness, he answered "the preacher has a God-given responsibility to study both the Word of God and the world of people."[8] To neglect either one will greatly decrease his qualifications as communicator of the Word. Dr. Anthony Evans, in an address at the 1986 Congress On Biblical Exposition called for preachers to exercise a "dual exegesis". "Dual Exegesis," he said, "requires that the expositor have the text of Scripture in the one hand and the newspaper in the other hand, accurately ascertaining its real needs and drawing the two together to continue the incarnation that was initiated by Christ. And so he ascertains the questions of the world and the truth of the Word — and brings them together."[9] Hearers who are before you each Sunday participate in humanity and all the needs and concerns of humanity. You enter that world to understand it only when you set down your theological works and pick up books and magazines that will assist in walking in modern man's shoes.

2. The preacher must also study the **records** of his congregation. He will find a wealth of valuable material in records. The membership records of the congregation will help him understand the age level of

the congregation so that he is aware what proportion of his audience is composed of youth facing the great decisions of life, young families at formative stages, mid-life couples who must adjust to an "empty nest", and retirees who need a new challenge. The records of vocations found among members will give the pastor insight concerning the issues they face, the pressures they feel, the temptations they encounter, and the level at which they are able to deal with the issues of the Christian faith. The records of baptisms, professions of faith, marriages, divorces, "early" deaths, and deaths from old age will give great insight into the concentration of "turning point" experiences that mark his audience. The records of stewardship will give him insight concerning generosity or lack of it and introversion or concern for the world-wide mission of the church. The records of the previous pastor's preaching will give insight about the character and concentration of his ministry so that he may be able to note what gaps have been left untouched and subjects that may have been overemphasized.

3. Consider also **reports of others.** We said that because of the size of many congregations and their increasing complexity, it is necessary for the preacher to draw on the impressions and information others are able to share. Chuck Swindoll, pastor of the large First Evangelical Free Church of Fullerton, California, told an audience that he relies heavily on his staff of 12-15 people to regularly provide feedback for him.[10] Joel Nederhood, television preacher on "Faith 20" Broadcast of CRC-TV, explains that he has the practice of beginning his day by reading the reports of the telephone counselors so that he can identify with concerns viewers have expressed.[11] Reuel Howe suggests forming feedback-discussion groups in each congregation that, in the absence of the pastor, will formulate their expression of concerns and needs and how well they are being met. This allows for objective and free expressions which can be communicated to the pastor later.[12] The preacher who has a faithful and committed Board of Elders who are in touch with congregational needs will be blessed richly by their assistance and insights. Some churches practice periodic visits by the Elders to the members of the congregation in their homes to minister

to them at times other than when a major need arises. Such Elders are
particularly valuable to the pastor who wants to learn of the needs of
his people. As I will show later, no pastor can know his congregation
as well as he ought without the assistance of his Board of Elders.

4. However, the most direct information for the pastor will come
through personal contact with the members of his congregation in
which he learns to **listen.** He must resist the temptation to isolate himself in his study. He needs as much direct contact with his people as
with his books. Halford Luccock counsels preachers to develop both a
"microscopic eye for individuals" as well as a "telescopic vision of
world trends."[13] He also counsels "...an unsleeping consciousness of
people, the habitual sounding of an alert in the presence of people,
something of a woodman's eye for tracks or movements in the
forest."[14] He puts it most pointedly when he says that the preacher
ought to be alert to two Trinities—the Father, Son and Holy Spirit and
also Tom, Dick and Harry!

Therefore, the pastor, who wants to learn about his people, will
value friendships with parishioners that enable him to walk in their
shoes. He will be a participant in small groups in the church so that he
can be in touch with their concerns. He will call on the members in
their homes to learn of their joys as well as sorrows. He will include
counseling as a part of his ministry and through such counseling will
learn of their crises. He will be present in hospitals and rest homes so
that from the bedside he may learn his parishioner's fears and weaknesses. Times of crises and emergency will prove to be some of the
most fertile areas for learning their needs.

Henry Sloan Coffin once said, "When a minister begins a week
with the feeling that he is 'preached out,' let him spend an afternoon...in going from family to family, and asking himself, 'what is
the spiritual need here? What guidance or comfort or awakening or
sharpening of conscience or enrichment in God ought this home or
this individual to receive?' "[15] If he will be a pastor "with" the people,
he will come to know them and be able to lead them better. To benefit
from such contacts he must discipline himself to be a good listener.

It's especially easy for preachers to talk all the time, but those who learn to be listeners in direct personal contact with people will be preparing well for preaching.

However, a preacher must learn to record and digest what he hears or it will soon be lost. Haddon Robinson suggests that the preacher jot down notes each day of what he has observed in the passing parade of people with whom he has had contact. Some pastors solicit suggestions and comments from the congregation concerning subjects that need to be addressed in preaching. Some find it helpful (and interesting) to solicit suggestions from the congregation for a series of summer messages entitled "Sermons You Asked For". Some time ago I put an insert in our weekly bulletin explaining that I was planning my preaching schedule for the coming year and asking, "What issues do you believe need to be addressed in sermons during the next year?" I received 129 suggestions and comments, showing a general pattern, and some of them very interesting indeed!

DISCOVERIES

For what does the preacher look as he engages in all this analysis? Obviously he can become overwhelmed with information and impressions. He must have some pattern for correlating everything and drawing conclusions from it.

He will want to gain an accurate description of the congregation. As the Discipline of Rhetoric and Public Speaking taught us, the preacher will benefit from information that informs him of the age range in his audience, of their national/ethnic background, of their intelligence level, of their interest in the subject, their relation to him, their emotional relation to the occasion, and their preparation for this occasion. It will also help him to draw conclusions about their convictions, religiously and politically.

He will also be interested in drawing conclusions about the diversity and the intensity of their needs. Harold W. Roupp once conducted a study of life-situations and attempted to classify 4000 responses to the question: "What is the outstanding question (problem or difficulty)

which you face in your thinking and living?" In studying 4000
responses he lists four major categories of concern; (1) the individual
and his inner self, (2) the individual in relation to his family, (3) the
individual in relation to larger groups and society, and (4) the individual in relation to God and the universe.[16] The Preacher must observe
his congregation with these concerns in mind.

Edgar N. Jackson, in his book *How To Preach To Peoples Needs,*
deals with the sixteen needs he considers most pressing: guilt, sorrow,
fear, alcohol, insecurity, loneliness, defeat, anger, doubt, tension, sickness, inferiority, injurious habits, aging, immaturity, and family problems.[17]

Martin Marty graphically describes the diversity of need in the typical congregation this way:

> All of the Seven Deadly Sins are present in each and all the people.
> Here are the pregnant, the repressed, the abandoned, the self-aban-
> doned, the promiscuous, those with secrets, those who have told all
> the secrets, those with lifted faces and those with face lifts, those
> who look as if they have problems and those who, by not looking as
> if they have problems, show that they do. Who else participates?
> Those who want to be reached out to during the Kiss of Peac-
> e—reached out to? They need to be kissed and would kiss—and
> those who cringe when nothing more than the Greeting of Peace
> calls for crisp handshakes and sullen greetings. Those who can stay
> for coffee hour and those who will covertly make their way away.
> The saints. The heroes. The louses. There is something of each in
> all, and though the sociologists type them as all one kind, they have
> astonishing sides to show.[18]

So the preacher will deliberately study his congregation to learn of
their diversity. He will insist on being jerked out of his tendency to
view them all as "common man". He will look for their "sides". While
doing so, he will observe that there are different classes of people
before him on Sunday morning, another consideration that forces him
to avoid the assumption that all are the same. Phillips Brooks said he
looks for (1) those prominent persons who peculiarly represent the
church to the world, (2) those supercilious hearers who come to
church for some reason but are out of sympathy with what goes on

there, (3) those who come purely out of habit seeking only respectability, and (4) those who are earnest seekers after truth.[19]

William Perkins, one of the fathers of Puritan Preaching, found six classes of people in the congregation. He divided them into two groups with three subgroups in each. First there are the unconverted, and such a class involves those who are spiritually indifferent and need arousing, those who are spiritually conceited and need humbling, and those who are humble, anxious, and seeking, and need to be led into the kingdom of God. There are also the converted, and this class involves the young children who need to be built up, the Christian under temptation and troubled who needs to be supported, and the mature Christian who needs help to advance in the faith.[20] Lloyd Perry sets up his categories a little differently when he says, "The effective biblical preacher should analyze his audience, which normally has four segments of people, in terms of attitudes toward him and his message. As well as believers, it includes apathetic people, people with doubts, and usually some people who are hostile to the gospel."[21]

Therefore, to assist in understanding the make-up of the congregation and their diverse needs, the preacher ought to live with a list of questions such as these:

1. What areas have been neglected in previous pulpit treatment?
2. What trends do I observe in the lives of this community that need addressing?
3. What potential problems lie just beneath the surface of lives here?
4. What underdeveloped areas of christian living are here?
5. In what areas of christian truth is their understanding weak?
6. What enemies of the christian faith are present and need to be attacked?
7. What basic issues are these people deeply concerned about?
8. What are their areas of indifference in which they need to be aroused?
9. What are their sharpest hurts and anxieties?
10. What are the subjects and areas about which they are defensive

and touchy?
11. At what points do they maintain prejudices and biases?
12. Do they have some hidden agendas that show up when they meet together?

Engaging in such a search will lead to very helpful discoveries that will make it possible to more accurately understand the congregation.

ADAPTATION

Now, with that understanding in mind, the preacher is ready to carry on a pulpit ministry to that congregation that will engage their attention and prove to be much more effective. It will be the kind of pulpit ministry that God had in mind when He called him there. Because he is aware of the contemporary situation in the lives and hearts of his people, his heightened sensitivity will give a greater ability to encode his message (to use Nida's terminology) in ways that will assure him that their decoding of it will be more reliable and accurate.

Awareness of their contemporary situation will convince the preacher that the message Christ and the Apostles proclaimed twenty centuries ago must be preached in a way that fits the mentality, culture, and experiences of people today.

Adaptation must never compromise the message. Preachers must not make concessions on essential truths or morals. They must not interpret the message in a way contradictory to its revealed and supernatural purpose just so they may be heard more favorably. However, they must fashion presentations of the unchanging truth for more meaningful communication with a changing people.

A preacher's goal must be to tailor-make the unchanging truth so that it may communicate well today. That will involve (1) selecting a well thought-through purpose for each message on the basis of the congregation's needs, (2) selecting subject material that is appropriate to the occasion and the congregation's state of mind and heart, (3) selecting rhetorical tools such as words, terminology, illustrations and sentence structure, that takes into consideration the capabilities of the congregation in mind, (4) organizing the message in a way that is appropriate to their frame of mind and intellectual capacity, and (5) selecting an appropriate length for his sermon.

Fosdick once gave us a glimpse into the process of adaptation as it took place in his preparation for preaching.

> Uniformly I am through with my manuscript on Friday noon. The next stage is one of the most important of all, for, fearful that in working out my subject I may have occasionally forgotten my object, and may have gotten out of the center of focus the concrete personalities who will face me on Sunday, I sit down on Saturday morning and re-think the whole business as if my congregation were visibly before my eyes, often picking out individuals and character- istic groups of individuals, and imaginatively trying my course of thought upon them, so as to be absolutely sure that I have not allowed any pride of discussion or lure of rhetoric to deflect me from my major purpose of doing something worthwhile with peo- ple. This process often means the elision of paragraphs that I like very much when I first wrote them and the rearrangement of order of thoughts in the interest of psychological persuasiveness.[22]

To be sure, this is a large task that greatly increases the responsibili- ties of the preacher. But, after all, he does not preach because it is easy. He preaches to release a burden in his heart — to effectively communicate God's unchanging truth in the midst of a rapidly chang- ing world.

Such a large task, however, cannot be done by a preacher who sits in his study all day, or by a preacher who moves to a new congrega- tion every few years, or by a preacher who allows people to build walls he cannot penetrate to see behind the scenes of their lives. A preacher left to do this work all by himself will fail. He must be a preacher with a broad world of books, friends, conversations, calling, counseling and listening. Even then, he needs the assistance of other capable, observant, mature people in the congregation and the people most likely and most uniquely suited to assist him in that role are the Elders.

The congregation with a preacher who takes this double task seri- ously, who studies both the Word of God and the world of his listen- ers, and who is assisted by Elders who provide their insight will be a congregation that can expect to hear relevant and appropriate messages.

1. Phillips Brooks, *Lectures on Preaching,* (Grand Rapids; Baker, n.d.), p. 190.

2. Ibid.

3. Catherine Marshall, *A Man Called Peter,* (New York: McGraw-Hill, 1951,), p. 196.

4. Robert T. Oliver, Rupert L. Cortright, Cyril F. Hager, *The New Training For Effective Speech* (New York: Dryden Press, 1946), pp. 283-286.

5. Loren Reid, *First Principles of Public Speaking* (Columbia, Missouri: Artcraft Press, 1962), p. 72.

6. Lionel Crocker, *Public Speaking For College Students* (New York: American Book Co., 1941), p. 303.

7. Ibid., p. 304.

8. Peter H. Eldersveld, "Our Preaching And Our World", an address delivered at the Christian Reformed Ministers' Institute at Calvin college, Grand Rapids, MI, June 8, 1961.

9. Anthony Evans, "The Demands for Relevancy," an address at the Congress On Biblical Exposition, at Anaheim, California, March 5, 1986.

10. Charles Swindoll, "Preparing A Bible Lesson", a taped lecture.

11. Expressed by Dr. Nederhood in a lecture on "Preaching And the Media" at Westminster Theological Seminary in California, January, 1986.

12. Reuel Howe, *Partners in Preaching,* (New York; Seabury Press, 1967), p. 36.

13. Halford E. Luccock, *In The Minister's Workshop,* (New York: Abingdon, 1944), p. 61.

14. Ibid., p. 79.

15. Henry Sloane Coffin, *What To Preach* (New York: Harper and Bros., 1926)

16. Harold W. Ruopp, "Life-Situation Preaching" (Part II), *The Christian Century Pulpit,* XII, June, 1941, p. 140-141.

17. Edgar N. Jackson, op. cit.

18. Martin Marty, *The Word,* (Philadelphia: Fortress Press, 1984), p. ,82, 83.

19. Phillips Brooks, op. cit., p. 190-202.

20. William Perkins, *The Art of Preaching,* n.a.

21. Lloyd Perry, "Preaching With Power And Purpose," *Christianity Today,* February 2, 1979, p. 23.

22. Harry E. Fosdick, in *If I Had Only One Sermon To Prepare,* ed. Joseph F. Newton, (New York: Harper and Brothers, 1932), p. 112-113.

CHAPTER FOUR

Adaptation In
The Gospels

W hat we have been talking about in the previous pages is not
some new discovery. The importance of understanding the
needs of the audience and adapting our communication
accordingly is a time-honored practice. We have seen it as a part of the
ancient practice of Rhetoric. A study of the history of Christian
preaching will also show that nearly all effective pulpiteers paid close
attention to their audience.

We see adaptation on the pages of the Holy Scriptures. Christ illustrates it; so do the apostles; the Old Testament prophets give evidence
of carefully honing their prophetic presentations to the needs and
experiences of their hearers. Because these writers were uniquely
inspired by the Holy Spirit in making their presentations, their practices in this regard take on increased significance. While they never
accommodated the content of the message, they certainly adapted the
form of the message and the method of its presentation to particular
audiences. In this chapter I will show from the New Testament that
our insistence on understanding our audience and crafting our message to meet their circumstances and needs follows as inspired biblical
precedent.

As we enter a study of the New Testament we discover that it is not easy to distinguish between informal conversations and more formal discourses. There is often overlap between the two. Where shall we draw the line? By the length of the record of it, say, perhaps, one paragraph qualifying as piece of a conversation, and more paragraphs becoming a discourse? Or does a conversation include two people and a discourse a group of people? But, then, what about a conversation in a small group setting, or perhaps a discourse to a small group? Is one a teaching setting and the other a relational setting? But do not both conversations and discourses contain elements of relationship and teaching? Is the one monologic and the other dialogic? Some discourses certainly include a dialogic character. To ask these questions helps us to realize that we are dealing with a continuum rather than neatly separated categories. In the final analysis we must live with the conclusion that we cannot finally and firmly draw the line between conversation and discourse.

There is no loss, however, in finding ourselves unable to definitively separate the two. The principles for both are the same. All good conversation is dialogic in character and therefore must exhibit sensitive understanding of and adaptation to the thoughts and needs of the other. More formal discourses must operate on the same principles as extended conversation in order to achieve effectiveness.However, we will focus on those passages which most clearly bear the marks of more formal discourse, while understanding that a fine line exists. Some of those discourses will be spoken, as Christ's addresses in the Gospels, and Paul's addresses in the Acts of the Apostles. Other discourses will be found written in the epistles.

MULTIPLE GOSPELS

We should begin by examining the fact that there are four gospel accounts included in our New Testaments. Have you ever wondered why so? Is it just because four records of the same life are bound to be more complete than one record? Is it because the Holy Spirit didn't trust each of the writers individually and needed the assurance that what one forgot another would be sure to include? Is it a New Testament illustration of the proverb of Ecclesiastes 3:12 that "A cord of three strands is not quickly broken," and four is better yet? No, the explanation for four gospel accounts is to be found in the diversity of the world to which the gospel writers were speaking, and the distinct audience that each had in mind. The multiplicity of gospels is itself a clear instance of audience adaptation.

Mark's Gospel, nearly all agree, was the earliest. Mark, a Jew who had very close associations with Peter, wrote in order to provide the people of Rome a summary of Peter's preaching. Mark, therefore, selected his material in a way that would present Jesus as a mighty conquering Savior King to whom all should turn in humble faith. His writings, in keeping with the Roman spirit and mind, exhibit chronological orderliness, a vividness of style that sparkles with action-packed decisiveness and miracle stories.

Matthew, however, was writing with another purpose and audience in mind. He was a Jew writing for Jews, aiming to more fully win them for Christ. He had his homiletical and literary eye on gaining those who are still unconverted and strengthening those who were already converted. His style, thought, and language patterns were, therefore, much more Hebraistic in character than Mark's. Matthew emphasized Jesus as the long-awaited Messiah of the Hebrew Old Testament Scriptures, and began his account with the record of genealogies. In his account we find at least forty Old Testament quotations, references he knew would be influential with readers who knew the Old Testament and accepted it as authoritative in character.

In contrast to Matthew who was a Jew writing for Jews, Luke was a non-Jew writing for non-Jews, probably Greeks. He began by explaining that his immediate purpose was to provide instruction and spiritual nurture for a Greek named Theophilus who, if not a believer, must certainly have been an interested inquirer (Luke 1:4). We sense, then, that his purpose was much broader than Matthew's for Luke aimed to enlighten earnest inquirers and believers, especially from the Greek-speaking Gentile world. That is why we find Luke using classical

Greek in his preface (1:1-4). In addition the character of Luke's presentation is quite different. He presented Jesus as the perfect or ideal man, constantly relating his narrative to contemporary historical events, and emphasized Christ's tender love and far-reaching sympathy more than the other gospels.

John, on the other hand, had a much different purpose than the other three Gospel-writers. He was even more explicit than the others in explaining his intended purpose. He admits to his selectivity in writing. Near the end of his Gospel he says: "Jesus did many other miraculous signs in the presence of his disciples..."[1] about which he could have written. In his closing verses he even says that Jesus did so many other things that if he had chosen to include them all "... I suppose that even the whole world would not have room for the books that would be written."[2] In chapter 20:31 he gives us the basic principle on the basis of which he made his selections: "But these are written that you may believe that Jesus is the Christ, the Son of God, and that by believing you may have life in his name." His purpose, therefore, was not to write a complete biography, nor merely to duplicate what the other Gospel writers had done, but to supplement their material in such a way that Christ's Messianic office and declared deity would be set forth in the most exalted terms. John's Gospel focuses, therefore, on miracles that proclaim Jesus' divine power, discourses that proclaim his mission, and places its greatest emphasis on the events and discourses of the last twenty-four hours before the crucifixion.

It can be seen, then, that in providing us with four Gospel accounts the Holy Spirit, as Inspirer, was adapting the material to widely differing audiences.

CHRIST'S DISCOURSES IN MATTHEW

Much of the record we have of Christ's ministry is dominated by conversations oriented to the conflict between Christ and the Pharisees. Such dialogue is obviously two-way, and carefully constructed to meet the situation, concerns, and needs of the other partici-

pants. In such conversations we meet a Christ who is always addressing a specific set of circumstances and concerns, with each response
formed by previous comments.

There are six major discourses of Christ in Matthew. Other Gospel
accounts contain fragments of these discourses, as well as some other
discourses, but it will serve our purpose to examine Matthew's
account of these six discourses to observe how Christ practiced the
principle of audience adaptation.

The first major discourse we have come to know as the "Sermon
On The Mount" contained in Matthew 5-7. To be in tune with how
Christ has adapted his presentation here we must remember that
Matthew's Gospel was written for Jews who were familiar with and
accepted the authority of the Old Testament Scriptures. We must also
remember that the key concern of Christ in this discourse is found in
Matthew 5:20, "For I tell you that unless your righteousness surpasses
that of the Pharisees and the teachers of the law, you will certainly not
enter the kingdom of heaven." He is therefore, addressing a Jewish
community under the strong influence of religious leaders who are
teaching a system of righteousness inferior because of its legalism.
Notice how Jesus begins. He speaks of "blessedness" (MAKARIOI)[3]
to people who were very familiar with the concept of SHALOM from
the Old Testament writings. He selects their concepts and language
and steps into their thought patterns, but then he quickly moves to
confrontation and correction as necessary and in six instances we hear
him saying, "You have heard...but I tell you..."[4] This is an effective
tactic by which he shows acquaintance with the traditions they have
been taught, and his determination to force a re-examination of those
teachings in order to correct them. Additionally, in chapters 6 and 7 he
demonstrates a keen awareness of current Jewish practices and the
constant threat of hypocrisy and addresses those matters directly. He
teaches them about prayer and fasting in a manner that contradicts the
practices and exposes the hypocrisy of their leaders.[5] He teaches them
about trusting in contrast to the preoccupation of their Gentile neigh-
bors with material pursuits.[6] He warns about false prophets and strik-

ingly shows his in-depth understanding of their religious milieu and the threats it involves for them.[7]

The second major discourse is found in Matthew 10 and includes Jesus' comments to the twelve when he sends them out in his name. The situation is described in verses 1-5 in which we are led to understand that this is a special event in which authority is being conveyed to the twelve so that they will be able to preach his message and also "...drive out evil spirits and to cure every kind of disease and sickness."[8] Consequently, the address to his disciples is not an abstract lecture about the kingdom of God, but a concrete presentation, packed with specific instructions about what they must do, what they can expect to face, and how they must be able to respond.

In Matthew 13, where Christ's third major discourse is recorded, we find Jesus in a much more public situation. Conflict and controversy have been developing. Chapter 12 records a sharp exchange between Jesus and the Jewish leaders about casting out demons by Beelzebub, and Jesus' retort about the unpardonable sin.[9] Crowds are aroused. He refers to them as a "wicked and adulterous generation".[10] Then he presents a series of seven parables, all of which are carefully groomed to correct their ideas about the kingdom of God, highlight the importance of receiving that kingdom by faith, and expose the destructive and corrupting influences of religious leaders in the community.[11]

In Matthew 18, where the fourth discourse is found, we discover that Jesus is alone with his disciples, and they are filled with questions after their experiences during Jesus' transfiguration. That event of transfiguration must have been striking and startling. Peter, James, and John, who shared it intimately with Jesus, must undoubtedly have explained it to the others. It was an experience they would love to have preserved permanently. Peter even suggested putting up some shelters so they could remain. However when they got back down the mountain things were different. They couldn't even heal an epileptic boy, and Jesus charged them with having little faith.[12] After the highs and the lows of those experiences, the disciples and Jesus were alone again and they raised some questions about greatness in the kingdom.[13] Jesus used that setting to speak to them pointedly by placing a child among them and using that child to impress on them the need for humility in service. He then spoke to them through a couple of parables designed to teach them about the need for reconciliation.[14] The joy of the transfiguration and the frustration of the unhealed epileptic had apparently made them particularly teachable for such lessons at that point. Jesus knew that.

Perhaps the harshest discourse of all is found in Matthew 23. Jesus was conscious of three groups of people around him; his disciples who must learn religious leadership, the crowds who are alternately attracted and then repelled, and, perhaps a little more in the background, the hypocritical religious leaders. Conscious of all three, and aware that such hypocritical leaders possess great destructive influence in the community, Jesus launched into a strongly worded and carefully crafted denunciation of the teachers of the law and Pharisees. "Woe to you!" he exclaimed seven times.[15] "You hypocrites!" he exclaimed six times.[16] "Blind guides",[17] "blind fools",[18] "white-washed tombs",[19] and "brood of vipers"[20] are the aggressive weapons that he used in his unrestrained attack. Jesus' method was to warn his followers about the dangers present, confront the false leaders courageously, make it clear that confrontation and conflict is unavoidable, and then express his compassionate concern for Jerusalem. He ended this confrontational discourse by informing them that the end is near: "you will not see me again until you say, 'blessed is he who comes in the name of the Lord'."[21]

The two chapters following contain the final discourse of Christ in this Gospel. The setting was the same as that of chapter 23. Jesus was in Jerusalem, involved in great conflict with false religious leaders, burdened by the unwillingness of Jerusalem to accept him, and while leaving the Temple area found the disciples beginning to question him more earnestly about all this.[22] He took that opportunity to speak candidly with them about the signs of the times, the promise of his return, the suddenness of such events, the urgency of their preparedness and the reality of judgment in order that they might not be disturbed by all that was about to happen. Within chapters 24 and 25 we hear him making predictions about coming difficulties, giving promises about his glorious return, instructing them about an apathy to avoid, telling parables to stimulate their concern for readiness and describing the drama of the judgment scene.

By analyzing these discourses we discover that Jesus used no stereotyped mode of address. He can speak of blessedness to those who follow him, can challenge those who must rise to a large mandate, can confront those who are dangerous hypocrites, can instruct with parables to overcome ignorance, and can prepare disciples for tumultuous events about to begin. He can speak their language, address their issues, expose their faults, and prepare them for what is about to take place. He can speak with a child on his lap, but he can also point a sharp finger at hypocrites. This means one thing—He knew well the circumstances and setting in each instance, and the persons in it, and crafted his discourse to meet that situation best.

CHRIST'S PATTERN IN THE OTHER GOSPELS

Is Matthew's representation of the methodology of Jesus isolated? Is it possible that he superimposed it on the ministry of Christ for some purpose? A look at the other Gospels makes it clear that he didn't. They too confront us with the same methodology. Christ, throughout his ministry, addressed his followers and his opponents in terms of their situation. That was characteristic of his entire ministry. A look at the other Gospels will verify that.

Consider several passages in the Gospel according to Mark. In chapter 1:16 and 17 Jesus meets Simon and Andrew while they were practicing their chosen vocation of fishing. Mark notes two things in presenting this situation. "They were fishermen", he says.[23] Then he notes that Jesus presented his call to Simon and Andrew in a figure of speech that reflects his understanding that, up to that point, fishing had been most important in their lives. "Come, follow me, and I will make you fishers of men", Jesus says.[24] That was masterful!

Mark 4 includes the parable that we've come to know as "The Parable of The Sower". In this instance, Mark does not choose to give us situational information, but a reading of the parable readily reveals it. Jesus was obviously addressing the matter of receiving the Word of God because "the crowd" that was gathered around him, though hearing the Word of God, was not receiving it properly. Jesus' intended point is stated in the words, "He who has ears to hear, let him hear"[25] In order to do justice to Jesus' intent, the parable should not be referred to as "The Parable of the Sower" but rather as "The Parable of the Four Soils" or "The Parable of Receiving the Word".

Later in that chapter, Mark provides a little commentary that helps understand Jesus' methodology. Jesus used parables as an effective tool for communicating the truth of God. But Mark points out that he told them "...as much as they could understand."[26] That statement implies a great diversity in their ability to hear and understand, and that Jesus took that into consideration in determining how much he said and how he said it. Also Mark tells us that Jesus understood that both the need and the capacity of the disciples was greater and so he continued his instruction to them in private.[27]

In Mark 7 we have opportunity to listen in on a discourse concerning matters of religious ceremony and the traditions of men that Jesus considered improper. Criticisms by the Pharisees of Jesus' disciples precipitated this discourse, and Jesus did not hesitate to confront them about their empty and irreligious practices.[28] It is interesting to note that in this instance Jesus appealed directly to the crowd so he would be sure they understood what he was saying,[29] and then also entered into a more intimate discussion with the disciples about the same thing.[30]

One more example from Mark's writings will suffice. In chapter 12:1-12 Jesus tells a pointed "Parable of the Tenants" intended to expose the evil that occurs when disgruntled workers conspire to kill the son of the owner. The situation out of which this communication came is obvious. Plots to kill Jesus were increasing in intensity and this parable is Jesus' way of confronting that. It becomes clear that those involved knew it was pointed at them and they reacted with both anger and fear.[31]

Turn to Luke's Gospel account and you will notice much of the same. The passage in Luke 4 in which Jesus revealed himself in the synagogue shows how Jesus adapted himself to local practices. It was his custom, Luke tells us, to go to the synagogue and worship there. He was familiar with all Synagogue procedures and accepted them. So, according to normal customary procedure, among people who were looking for the Messiah (although rather dimly), he went to worship, read from the Scroll, sat down to expound on the Year of Jubilee, and then proceeded to proclaim its fulfillment in Himself. In the dialogue that followed, Luke shows us how Jesus even anticipated their objections ("Surely you will quote this proverb to me; 'Physician, heal yourself!' ") and the answers he gave to their anticipated responses. He even anticipated their resistance.[32]

In Luke 11:37-54, we find a discourse of Christ marked by six "woes". An analysis of its context will show us that this discourse was groomed to fit a context. Jesus had been engaged in debate with religious leaders who charged him with driving out demons in the name of Beelzebub. He spoke to them about hearing and obeying the Word of God and other matters. Soon after that Jesus entered the home of a Pharisee and immediately found himself in the middle of another debate concerning ceremonial cleansings. This conflict precipitated a stern and fierce confrontation with the Pharisees that we know as the "Six Woes". This confrontation ushers in a period of increased hatred and opposition for Jesus.

Another chapter where we see this practice exhibited is Luke 15. Here Luke carefully sets the situation and need before us in the first two verses: Tax collectors and "sinners" were gathering around him and muttering about his policies and practices. Jesus understood that they resented his willingness to receive and forgive sinners. So he addressed them in the form of three parables carefully crafted to illustrate how repentant sinners should be received. Here he used the story form, stressing in each instance that the shepherd, the woman, and the father are all eager to retrieve what is lost and experience great joy in finding. However Jesus did not end with the three parables, but expanded the final parable to include the brother who became angry and refused to join the celebration that was going on over his younger brother's return. This surprising twist at the end illustrates Jesus' craft of adaptive communication for he aimed it pointedly at those in his company who refused to receive repentant sinners.[33]

Three examples from the Gospel of John will suffice to show that John did not overlook such a technique of Jesus either. In chapter 4 John says Jesus was on his way back to Galilee and chose to pass through Samaria though that was out of the ordinary for Jews. His conversation with the woman at the well has been studied and analyzed by many as one of the most outstanding examples of relevancy and adaptation. Jesus masterfully moves the conversation from the water in the well to living water, from her record of five husbands to his claim of Messiahship, from Mt. Gerizim to worship in spirit and truth, and from physical food to the satisfaction Jesus finds in doing the will of God. It is a story that portrays a man with a deep sense of mission, a keen understanding of the circumstances and reactions within his hearers and an extremely effective ability to move conversation from earthly subjects to eternal concerns.

In John 5, Jesus was again embroiled in conflict with the Jewish leaders who are persecuting him. Their anger was increasingly aroused both by his sabbath practices and his self-revelation as the Son of God. Jesus refused to be intimidated and, in this instance, was less concerned about being palatable than answering them with bold declarations in which he identified himself as the Son of God through whom life is given, and who has received the right to exercise judgment from the Father. He must, therefore, be honored as the Son. He clearly pointed to himself as the Source of eternal life and drew upon five witnesses to that fact.[34]

The most concentrated material in John's Gospel is found in chapters 13-17 which deal in great depth with the communication between Jesus and the disciples on Thursday evening before his arrest. The scene began in the Upper Room with only Jesus and the disciples present, commemorating the Passover Meal. However, Jesus had several other concerns on his heart. He knew that the time was short and he would soon be crucified; he loved the disciples with an intense love; and was aware of a traumatic betrayal, an agonizing trial, and an indescribable crucifixion that would shortly occur. He used that setting, therefore, to teach the disciples about the matter of servanthood (by the washing of their feet[35]), to predict the betrayal (by dipping a piece of bread[36]), to minister to their fears ("Do not let your hearts be troubled"[37]), to continue to reveal himself ("...the way and the truth and the life"[38]), to call them to bear fruit ("...apart from me you can do nothing"[39]) and to warn them of the hatred of the world ("...it hated me first"[40]). He then concluded by explaining the reason why he wanted to say all those things. "I have told you these things, so that in me you may have peace. In this world you will have trouble. But take heart! I have overcome the world."[41]

SOME OBSERVATIONS

On the basis of our study of the Gospel records, several observations are in order concerning the ministry of Jesus and his method of communication.

(1) There is a keen awareness of the situation in which the hearers find themselves and how that affects their ability to receive the message. Each of the Gospel writers, we have seen, was very conscious of the particular audience to which they wanted to communicate, and the purpose they had for that communication. Jesus, too, was keenly in tune with the anger and objections of his opponents, the anxieties and needs of his disciples, and the dangers and threats that faced the ambivalent crowds.

(2) There is a consistency of content throughout the Gospels. Content was never compromised for the sake of communication. Adaptation is practiced; accommodation is not. The purpose of the Gospels is the revelation of Jesus Christ as the Son of God who came to bring life through death and resurrection. In writing to Romans,

Jews, Greeks and others, the authors never compromised their message. When Jesus dealt with disciples who were following him, religious leaders who hated him, and with crowds who just didn't know what to think, his message of self revelation was always the same.

(3) There is a variation of purpose. When the twelve disciples were sent out to preach and heal, Jesus gave them careful instruction and encouragement. When the crowds were about to be led astray by the hypocrisy of the Pharisees, Jesus compassionately warned them and pleaded with them. When the religious leaders stubbornly held to their empty and self-centered traditions, Jesus lashed out at them with woes that make all sincere souls tremble. When the disciples stood at the threshold of a frightening crucifixion, Jesus tenderly comforted and supported them.

(4) There is a careful choice in the selection of material. We heard Mark say that Jesus told them "as much as they could understand". John admitted that he was very selective. And Matthew included references intended to carry weight with Jews.

(5) Finally, there is an observable variation in style that results from sensitivity to the situation of the hearers. Jesus didn't just call the fishermen to follow him, he calls them to become "fishers of men". Mark wrote in an action-packed style to appeal to the Roman mind. Luke's Gospel emphasizes the compassionate material from the healings of Jesus. Jesus spoke to some groups in colorful parables, and to other groups with the venom of "woes", and then at another time wept over Jerusalem. All such variations are influenced by the situation in which the communication takes place and the factors that influence the hearing ability of the audience.

1. John 20:30
2. John 21:25
3. cf. Matthew 5:3-11
4. cf. Matthew 5:21 and 22, 27 and 28, 31 and 32, 33 and 34, 38 and 39, 43 and 44.
5. cf. Matthew 6:1-8 and 16-18
6. cf. Matthew 6:25-34
7. cf. Matthew 7:15-23

8. cf. Matthew 10:1

9. cf. Matthew 12:24-32

10. cf. Matthew 12:39

11. Note the parables of the Sower, of the weeds among the wheat, of the mustard seed, of the yeast, of the hidden treasure, of the fine pearls, and of the net of fish. All are found in Matthew 13.

12. cf. Matthew 17:19-21

13. cf. Matthew 18:1

14. Note the parable of the lost sheep in Matthew 18:10-14 and the parable of the unmerciful servant in Matthew 18:21-35.

15. cf. Matthew 23:13, 15, 16, 23, 25, 27, and 29.

16. cf. Matthew 23:13, 15, 23, 25, 27 and 29.

17. cf. Matthew 23:16.

18. cf. Matthew 23:17

19. cf. Matthew 23:27.

20. cf. Matthew 23:33.

21. cf. Matthew 23:39.

22. cf. Matthew 24:3.

23. Mark 1:16.

24. Mark 1:17

25. cf. Mark 4:9 and note their repetition in Mark 9:23,24.

26. Mark 4:26.

27. cf. Mark 4:34.

28. cf. Mark 7:1-13.

29. cf. Mark 7:14.

30. cf. Mark 7:30.

31. cf. Mark 12:12.

32. cf. Luke 4:20-27

33. cf. especially Luke 15:25-32 and note how the parable of the prodigal son could stand complete without this addendum. It was added, therefore, by the deliberate design of Christ to address a situation that needed attention.

34. cf. John 5:31-47 and note the five groups/classes of witnesses that he cites: (1) John the Baptist, (2) the work of Jesus, (3) the Father who sent Him, (4) the Scriptures, and (5) Moses.

35. cf. John 13:1-17.

36. cf. John 13:26,27.

37. cf. John 14:1-4.

38. cf. John 14:6.

39. cf. John 15:1-8.

40. cf. John 15:18.

41. cf. John 16:33

CHAPTER FIVE

Adaptation In The Epistles

S ince effective communication requires skillful adaptation to the audience, it should not surprise us that Jesus' ministry exhibits such a practice. He was a master at sensing the needs of his audience and grooming the form of his message to their particular situation.

But what of the remainder of the New Testament? It too offers insight and proof concerning the importance of adaptation. Paul occupies the center of our attention in the remainder of the New Testament and his ministry is the source of great encouragement in becoming adept at adaptation. Luke's record of Paul's major discourses in the book of Acts exhibits his use of such adaptation, while Paul's own epistolary writings provide additional examples of the same. As a matter of fact, in a number of epistles we hear him speaking directly about adaptation and even explaining the principles he follows. However the practice is not uniquely Pauline. Several other New Testament writers give evidence of the same approach.

By the time we have covered these materials, our hypothesis concerning the need for adaptation will be very well substantiated. Then we must move on to the task of answering the question that urgently presents itself, "How is it to be accomplished?"

DISCOURSES OF PAUL

A great deal of Luke's material in Acts covers the eight major discourses of Paul on his missionary journeys. Here we see Paul in
action, and we are able to feel the dynamic of his intense efforts to
communicate the gospel of Jesus Christ to Jew and Gentile alike. In
several instances these are sermons as we normally think of them, and
in other instances they are more broadly considered discourses and
speeches. Some take place in a worship setting while others are public
speeches.

Those who have carefully studied and analyzed these discourses
have noted that one of the prominent features of Paul's messages is the
"…total adaptation of his message to the particular audience before
him."[1] Indeed, "Every aspect of his preaching is deliberately suited to
the hopes, needs, and understandings of his immediate listeners;"[2] and,
"Every choice (Paul) makes is guided by the nature of his immediate
audience, and every aspect of his preaching is suited to their unique
needs."[3]

Jay E. Adams has done an extensive analysis of the eight discourses
of Paul as recorded in Acts and presents us with very helpful material.

> It is my unproven hypothesis that Luke selected these particular ser-
> mons and speeches partly on the basis of the variety of audiences
> and situations, not to show Paul's ability to adapt, but to demon-
> strate the remarkable way in which the gospel of Christ spread to all
> sorts and conditions of men. But Paul's avowed advocacy of the
> principle of adaptation together with an extant body of materials
> presented to widely differing groups of people, yet consisting of one
> and the same message, also provided an ideal combination of fac-
> tors for just such a study.[4]

It is not our purpose in the present study to examine each of the
eight discourses in detail, but to note that because of the variation of
audience and circumstances Paul's method of presentation varies. Paul
spoke to four types of audiences.

1. The Congenial Audience

In Acts 20:16-38 we observe Paul addressing an audience that is
obviously most congenial, one with whom Paul had the warmest of

relationships. When this veteran and highly respected missionary pastor has the opportunity to speak with the Elders from Ephesus, who had undoubtedly been brought into the Christian Church through his ministry, we expect evidence of a warm and personal attachment between them. The fact that he meets with them at Miletus on his way to Jerusalem, and that they all sense this is a farewell address, only adds to the intensity of the personal attachments. This audience is about the most consistently homogeneous one that Paul addresses. They are not only his converts, but also close and trusted personal friends who had worked side by side with him. As Elders in the church they shared Paul's concern for the welfare of the church and the threat of persecution. Such a situation is perhaps the easiest one in which to succeed with effective communication. However, it is to our benefit to note how Paul handles the situation. He recalls his ministry in Ephesus and recounts the labors he had invested in the church there, how he had been tested by the efforts of the Jews but continued to faithfully preach and teach there. Then he looks ahead to the ministry he would undertake in Jerusalem and what great uncertainties would be associated with it for he had been warned that hardship lay ahead. Then he carefully warns them about the dangers that they will face in the church, and includes an emotional appeal to be faithful to their task even in the most difficult of circumstances.[5] So here we see warning and challenge communicated in a context of warmth, love and reminiscence.

2. The Mixed Audience

In Acts 13, the situation is very different. Paul handles it quite differently. It is, perhaps, the best example of Paul's approach to a mixed audience. Paul is speaking here in the synagogue to Antioch. Traveling preachers were frequently given an invitation to address the synagogue congregation. This congregation was by no means homogeneous: some were Jews of the dispersion who had retained the principal tenents of their faith even though they had become somewhat hellenized, others were proselytes who had turned their backs on the polytheism of Greek culture and accepted the beliefs of Judaism. Even among these there was diversity for some had made a complete break with their previous culture and some had not. The situation, therefore, was marked by great diversity and the potential for tension was great. Paul skillfully adapts to this situation. He carefully identifies with his audience, calling them "brothers", while referring to God as "our Father", and drawing them together by the words "...children of Abraham and you god-fearing Gentiles".[6] He demonstrates his commitment to the authority of the teachings of the Scriptures with which they would have been familiar. Then he proceeds to point to Jesus Christ as the Messiah, the One from whom alone they can receive the forgiveness of sins.[7] This seems to have been extraordinarily effective; soon increasing crowds came to hear him and a church was established in that city with many converted Gentiles as members[8]. As a matter of fact the response was so overwhelmingly positive that it provoked an angry reaction from some of the Jews who began to stir up opposition against Paul and Barnabas.[9]

3. The Pagan Audience

From his address to a warm audience and a mixed audience, we turn to the scenes in Lystra and Athens in which he addresses pagan audiences. In Acts 14, at Lystra the influence of polytheism was still strong, and when Paul healed the lame man they were quickly ready to call Paul and Barnabas "gods". Lystra apparently was characterized by uneducated pagan peasants who had not been influenced by either the sophistication or the skepticism of Greek and Roman culture. Athens, in Acts 17, is also a pagan audience but of a quite different sort. Here Paul is dealing with the learned and intelligent, the Epicurean and Stoic philosophers, those who "...spent their time doing nothing but talking about and listening to the latest ideas."[10] So in both cities, Paul meets pagan audiences, one educated and one uneducated. Though both audiences are pagan, because they are so different Paul handles the two situations very differently. In Lystra he reacts with horror to their eagerness to declare them gods. He shouts, tears his clothes, and directly confronts them with sharp disapproval of what they are doing.[11] In spite of Paul's efforts to correct them, the crowd is not sympathetic to his point and are soon swayed to stone Paul and leave him for dead outside the city. In Athens we find him handling a pagan audience in an opposite manner. Here, in a masterful example of adaptation, he shows himself sensitive to their mixture of curiosity and hostility, disarms his opponents by speaking their language and citing their poets, earns a hearing by utilizing their style of speaking and vocabulary, and builds his presentation on the revelation of God through nature.[12] He is able thereby to gain their approval for a presentation of the gospel and presents the truths of judgment, resurrection, and the call to faith without arousing their animosity. The pagan audience in Lystra stoned him, but in the pagan audience in Athens there was at least a number who said, "We want to hear you again on this subject."[13]

4. The Hostile Audience

When we meet Paul in Jerusalem, in Acts 21-23, we find him dealing with an outright hostile audience. He has returned from his missionary journeys and the issue of the conversion of the Gentiles is a volatile one. He is accused of bringing uncircumcised people into the Temple and the crowd is about ready to kill him when Roman soldiers intervene.[14] Under those tense circumstances he asks for the right to speak. The next day he is ushered before the Sanhedrin, hardly any less hostile, for there the two bitterly opposed factions of Pharisees and Sadducees both considered him to be the chief representation of this Christianity which they despised. How will this preacher who has found himself in so many different situations now be able to handle this one? His attempt reveals his personal understanding of the situation of the audience. He not only asks for the right to address them, but does so in Aramaic, stresses his Jewishness and common heritage with them, and, by recounting his conversion experience, reminds them that he once believed and acted as they.[15] He is careful, in the process, not to further inflame the situation but never succeeds in calming them and as a result finds himself the next day before the Sanhedrin to make his defense. Here his strategy undergoes a change. He apparently knew that he would not be able to win them all, and so in terms of his careful and insightful understanding of them and their weaknesses, he decides to divide them. Clearly identifying himself as a Pharisee, he sees such discord break out between the Pharisees and the Sadducees that they are not able to function as a unified group.[16] Apparently, in the process, he gained at least some hearing for the matter of a resurrection of the dead, but also succeeded in eliminating unified hatred and judgment against himself.

In the final two discourses in Acts, we find Paul in the courtroom facing the civil authorities (chapters 24-26). He appears before Felix first, then Festus and Agrippa. Serious charges have been made by the Sanhedrin and must be adjudicated. Here as he gives his own defense, we discover that he functions somewhat differently than he had before an audience to whom he wanted to preach the gospel. We find him here (particularly before Felix) making a straightforward, very direct, defense as would normally occur in a courtroom. He makes it clear that the opposition has no hard evidence and has no credible witnesses to present. His defense is refined and intelligent, persuasively recounting once again his own conversion, speaking directly to the heart of Agrippa in doing so.[17]

It has not been our purpose here to examine each of these discourses in great detail, but to note Paul's adaptability in them. His audiences were very diverse; some warm, some hostile, some pagan, and some mixed. With changing audiences, we see changing methods of presentation. To some he spoke directly and straightforwardly making a persuasive defense. To others he spoke reminiscently in review of their work together. To others he reacted with confrontation and rebuke, while to still others he built on their authorities and used their language to gain a hearing. In all such events he demonstrates sensitivity to the situation of the audience, their needs, their disposition, and exhibits his own skillful ability to adapt. In it all, he never compromised the content of his message.

CORINTHIAN CORRESPONDENCE

In addition to the sermons and speeches of Paul which are recorded by Luke, his preserved correspondence with the Corinthian Church provides an excellent opportunity to gain insight into how Paul aimed to communicate. He wrote more to this church than any other. The circumstances in Corinth involved many difficulties, and this church has been known as Paul's "problem congregation." There were divisions within the church that required careful and deliberate attention; there were moral and ethical inconsistencies that needed immediate addressing. In addition, Paul and his apostleship had been attacked so directly on more than one occasion, attempting to discredit him, that he felt compelled to defend himself. Consequently, there was a significant flow of correspondence from Paul's pen to this congregation. The Scriptures preserve 29 chapters, but there is convincing evidence that he probably wrote two more letters. In I Corinthians 5:9 he says, "I have written you in my letter…" indicating that another letter has preceded I Corinthians. In II Corinthians 2:3 and 4 he speaks of another letter that he wrote "…out of great distress and anguish of heart and with many tears…" and II Corinthians 7:8 he speaks of the possibility that he has caused them sorrow by his letter, though he does not regret that. So apparently an even more stern and severe letter came their way between the two epistles that we presently have, in addition to a letter that preceded I Corinthians. Such extensive correspondence, even though we do not have all of it preserved, can certainly give us significant insight into his manner of addressing them in such circumstances.

As we analyze this correspondence, we are faced first with the fact that Paul obviously relied a great deal on reports that came to him, perhaps reports that were precipitated by investigations that he had encouraged. The presence of such reports, and the seriousness with which Paul took them, indicates that his correspondence was carefully formed by his awareness of their situation.

Immediately, in I Corinthians 1:10ff where he begins to address the matter of their disunity, he is careful to make it clear that he has been informed of the problem that exists. "My brothers, some from Chloe's household have informed me that there are quarrels among you."[18] This report is the basis for his attention to their disunity. By contrast, we note that in Ephesians 4:4-6 he teaches the Ephesians about the matter of Christian unity but does so more abstractly and theoretically, and not on the basis of a particular troublesome situation about which he has been informed. The treatment of unity in I Corinthians is carefully honed and pointed to their specific situation.

His treatment of two other major and potentially explosive subjects rests on the same basis. In I Corinthians 5, while treating the difficult subject of immorality among them, and their apparent tolerance of it, he notes: "It is actually reported..." In I Corinthians 6, where he treats the matter of brother meeting brother in a courtroom before unbelievers, he also makes it clear that he is addressing their situation: "The very fact that you have lawsuits among you..." So he is writing to them on the basis of his knowledge of their actual situation, not in abstract.

There is another pattern in this first epistle that reveals the same awareness. Six different times it becomes clear that he is addressing matters about which they have inquired either in writing or through verbal reports. He indicates repeatedly that he is answering inquiries: "Now for the matters you wrote about...," "Now to the unmarried and the widows...," "Now about the virgins...," "Now about food sacrificed to idols...," "Now about spiritual gifts..." and "Now about the collection for God's people..."[19] We also hear him saying, "...I hear that when you come together as a church, there are divisions among you, and to some extent I believe it."[20] These statements all give us the clear picture of an apostle very concerned about and aware of the situation in Corinth who aims to address that situation directly. So the content selected as subject material is formed by their situation and not merely by what he has independently decided is appropriate.

Paul tips his hand a little further in I Corinthians 3:1-3 and acknowledges his conviction that their situation determines how much he can give them in instruction and exhortation. He apparently wanted to tell them so much more. The learned Paul, who seemed able to deal so comfortably with the great themes of profound Christian truth, is limited because of the immaturity of the Corinthian Christians. He wanted to address them as spiritual men who could handle great things, but because they were worldly, infants in the faith, he had to reduce their diet. He wanted to communicate solid food to them, but they were capable of handling only milk. There is frustration in Paul's pen when he writes that, but he is wise enough to know that his efforts to communicate effectively must be molded by their ability to receive and not only his ability to give.

Perhaps the main passage in which Paul explains his desire to adapt for the sake of effective communication is I Corinthians 9:19-23. When he says, "...I make myself a slave to everyone, to win as many as possible", we know that we are hearing someone who intensely covets effective communication of the Christian Gospel. In order to understand fully what Paul intends to say here we must see that this paragraph is found in the broader context of a discussion concerning Christian liberty and the burning question of whether Christians ought to eat meat that has been sacrificed to idols. He concludes chapter 8 with the firm statement that he never wants any of his actions to cause his brother to fall into sin. In chapter 9 he explains that those who are committed to preach the gospel do have the right to receive their living from the gospel, but hastens to say that he has chosen to give up those rights. He preached without cost to them and served as a tent-maker while preaching. So here we see that he is willing to alter even his own personal situation in order to communicate better. First, he is willing to give up eating meat, and now he is willing to give up his right to receive his living from the gospel. Then, we are ready to hear what he is saying in 9:19-23. My purpose, he says, is to adapt my circumstances in such a way as will gain a greater hearing for the gospel. He points to changes he makes in his lifestyle for the sake of communication! He states the general principle in v.22 and 23. "I have become all things to all men so that by all possible means I might save some. I do all this for the sake of the gospel, that I may share in its blessings." He amplifies that principle in the following verses where he explains that it involves strict self-control and training, even beating his body and its impulses into submission so that he might never be disqualified. We hear him expressing himself more specifically in the application of that principle (verses 20 through 22). He has in view the importance of communicating the gospel to both the Jew and the Gentile, that is, to those under the law (or, who considered themselves to be under the law) and those who are not under the law. In order to accomplish that he is even willing to become weak (that is, with less discernment and greater restriction) for the sake of those who are weak, that is, the "weaker brothers" he has been concerned about.

We have been observing the practical application of this principle in our analysis of the discourses and letters of Paul. We have seen that to the Jews he speaks from the background of the Scriptures he knew they accepted; he identifies with their heritage; he cites their authorities; he avoids those matters that are provocative and explosive (such as the conversion of the Gentiles), and he repeats his personal conversion story. We have seen that he is also able to relate well to the Gentiles, speaking to them, as in Athens, on the basis of general revelation, citing the Greek poets, and framing his thoughts in words and thought patterns that are appropriate to them. He, therefore, proves himself to be an adaptable, flexible speaker.

However, we must make it clear that he was never willing to alter basic content. No accommodation of the truth would ever be found in Paul! He had made that clear to the Corinthians early in the second chapter. "For I resolved to know nothing while I was with you except Jesus Christ and him crucified."[21] His message might not be with wise and persuasive words, but it certainly would contain the true gospel of salvation in Jesus Christ. His statements to the Galatians were even stronger: "But even if we or an angel from heaven should preach a gospel other than the one we preached to you, let him be eternally condemned!"[22] "May I never boast except in the cross of our Lord

Jesus Christ."[23] Such statements are sufficient testimony of Paul's unwillingness to include an accommodation of the message as part of his techniques of adaptation.

Before we distill some principles from this study, I want to take a look at how a couple of other New Testament writers adapt to their audience. There is much debate concerning the authorship of Hebrews. Entering into that debate is beyond the scope of our present intentions. Whoever he was, he too found it necessary to adapt to communicate well. He is working intensively in the first five chapters to communicate truths about the preeminence of Jesus Christ as the eternal High Priest. There is great assurance and hope in those truths, and these Hebrew Christians, tempted as they are to abandon the faith and lapse back into Judaism, are in need of hearing about Christ's priestly function. Yet the author realized that he must contend with severe limitations. He must adapt to their slowness to learn and their need for assistance with the elementary truths of God's Word all over again. They are immature and can only handle milk, incapable of digesting the solid food that more mature folks relish. So, he says, even though "We have much to say about this (the priestly office of Christ)..." we will not do so because of the limitations of your abilities, for "...it is hard to explain because you are slow to learn." Instead of giving them the "solid food", about which he wished to write, he realized they are in need of "someone to teach (them) the elementary truths of God's Word all over again..."[24] Here, therefore, is another instance in which the writer limits selectively what he communicates because of the restricted capabilities of the readers. However, he does not leave that subject without exhorting them to go on to greater maturity!

One other interesting example of adaptation is found in Jude. This brother of Jesus was all excited about writing a general epistle to Christians in which he might reflect on the salvation in Jesus that they shared. I can imagine him jotting his thoughts down, planning to joyfully recount the riches of their salvation. He could imagine this loving, encouraging letter circulating among the churches and bringing good cheer to everyone. Such a letter, however, was not to be. News he had not counted on completely changed his thoughts and intentions, and consequently changed his epistle too. The news was about heresy, false teachers and the denial of the true faith. So he wrote. But as he began he explains how his planned epistle took an abrupt turn: "Dear Friends, although I was very eager to write to you about the salvation we share, I felt I had to write and urge you to contend for the faith that was once for all entrusted to the saints."[25]

SOME OBSERVATIONS

In our study of the Epistles we have made a number of observations that are appropriate to the method of adaptation that was practiced, particularly by Paul, and others too.

(1) We have observed that there must be a flexibility in the form of our presentation of the gospel that takes into account the circumstances and disposition of the audience before us. In one place, Lloyd-Jones put it this way: "The Apostle's argument, surely, is that there must be elasticity in our actual mode of presentation."[26]

(2) We have also observed that violence may never be done to the content of the message. The truth of the Christian Gospel is unalterable. All men, regardless of their circumstances, need to hear the truth. Though the form in which that truth is presented must be elastic, the truth is not.

(3) We must consider the level of understanding of our hearers. Christ told them only "as much as they could understand".[27] Paul found them too worldly to receive solid food and had to give them milk.[28] The author of Hebrews regretted that he could not tell them all he had to say because they were "slow to learn."[29]

(4) When error is present our message must be aimed to correct it. Jude found his plans changing when he heard about threats to the faith. Much of I Corinthians was written because of errors that needed correction: divisions, immorality, lawsuits, abuses of the Lord's Supper, and abuses in worship.

(5) We must be willing to adjust style, structure and vocabulary to

enter our listener's frame of references. The four Gospel writers have previously illustrated this. But Paul does also. We find him speaking with a different style in Lystra than in Athens. He addresses Felix differently than he does the hostile mob in Jerusalem.

(6) The mood of our presentation will vary greatly with the situation. Of the two letters to Corinth that have survived, we find the mood is quite different. I Corinthians is very confrontational, baring all the warts of the church, and showing the missionary's grieving heart. II Corinthians is much more personal and reveals a pastor's heart of love. One of the other Corinthian letters that has not survived must have been very severe and stern as Paul admits that in his preserved correspondence with them.

(7) Our selection of supportive materials will be greatly influenced by the situation of our audience. Paul's use of John the Baptist and the Old Testament Scriptures was effective with the folks in Antioch, but would have been useless in Athens. His reference to Greek poets was effective in Antioch, but would have been foolish with the hostile mob in Jerusalem.

1. "Patterns For Preaching: A Rhetorical Analysis", by Donald R. Sunukjian, cited in *Public Speaking: A Handbook for Christians*, by A. Duane Litfin, (Grand Rapids: Baker, 1981), p. 184.

2. ibid., p. 194.

3. ibid., p. 36, 37.

4. *Audience Adaptations in the Sermons and Speeches of Paul*, by Jay E. Adams, (Grand Rapids, Baker, 1976), p.i.

5. Note how in Acts 20:28-32 he uniquely combines a strong warning, a stirring challenge, and personal encouragement.

6. cf. Acts 13:26.

7. cf. Acts 13:26-41 and observe how Paul is uncompromising in his presentation of the gospel call regardless of his audience.

8. cf. Acts 13:42, 43.

9. cf. Acts 13:44,45.

10. Acts 17:21.

11. cf. Acts 14:14,15.

12. cf. Acts 17:22-31.

13. Acts 17:32.

14. cf. Acts 21:27-36.

15. cf. Acts 21:37-22:21.

16. cf. Acts 23:6-10.

17. cf. Acts 26:1-27.

18. I Corinthians 1:11.

19. cf. I Corinthians 7:1, 8, 25; 8:1, 12:1; and 16:1.

20. I Corinthians 11:18.

21. I Corinthians 2:2.

22. Galatians 1:8.

23. Galatians 6:14.

24. Hebrews 5:11, 12.

25. Jude 3.

26. *Preaching and Preachers,* by D. Martyn Lloyd-Jones, (Grand Rapids: Zondervan, 1971), p. 138.

27. Mark 4:33.

28. I Corinthians 3:1,2.

29. Hebrews 5:11.

CHAPTER SIX

Where Are The Elders?

I t ought to be clear by now that we have maneuvered the preacher into a very difficult situation. We've warned him that some sermons are effective, and others are not. We've pointed out that, historically, all good rhetoricians put a great deal of effort into understanding their audience, and urged the preacher to do the same. The average preacher at that point begins to feel the pressure of greater responsibility and more work in this already difficult business of preparing and preaching effective sermons. "My schedule is already full, my time is limited, and my energy even more limited," he complains. "How can I possibly find time for such analysis and evaluation? And besides, how am I supposed to go about this business of finding out what all the congregational needs are? I can't begin interviewing every member. I wouldn't have any time to write sermons!"

Also, we worsened his situation all the more by pointing out that both Christ and the Apostles set the pattern for us by engaging in thorough analysis and adaptation. By now the preacher may be tearing his hair out. He senses that preaching effective sermons is much more difficult and complex than he previously imagined. His sense of inadequacy skyrockets!

How will he respond to this pressure? Will he consider it a positive challenge that stirs him to a more careful study of his audience? Will he become motivated to analyze his hearers as carefully as he analyzes the Word he preaches to them? Will he find ways to rearrange his priorities so that room can be found in his schedule for more thorough evaluation? Or will he only find his frustration increasing all the more, and perhaps be tempted to either settle for lower standards or haul his kite down? I fear that the latter course may be adopted by those preachers whose congregations are rather large and, therefore, complex. For them it will be easy to say, "the job is too large to do it that carefully; my Sunday audience has too many faces; my responsibilities are already too heavy!"

But wait! There is hope! It is time to bring the elders into the picture! Here are your lifesavers! God never intended for you to carry out this task alone. The Scripture and the pattern of the early church exhibit a plurality of leadership. The pastor who, therefore, finds himself pursuing this work alone has lost sight of the assistance Christ intended.

However, the church today faces a serious deficiency because the office which is intended to provide such assistance does not function that way; most elders do not realize that their office involves the responsibility of assisting the preacher in understanding the needs and concerns of the congregation. In some quarters there is suspicion about such an office. In other quarters the office exists only in a severely underdeveloped form. And in still other quarters the office of elder does not exist at all.

I recently surveyed local colleagues in the ministry and discovered that nearly all indicated they would welcome greater assistance from their elders in understanding the needs and concerns of the congregation. However, as soon as they said that, many were just as quick to express their doubt about the willingness of their elders to provide such assistance.

In 1831, Samuel Miller, a clerk in the District of New Jersey of the Presbyterian Church, wrote "An Essay on the Warrant, Nature and

Duties of the Office of the Ruling Elder in the Presbyterian Church". In this pointed essay he claims,

> If the statement given in the following essay, concerning the duties incumbent on ruling elders be correct, it is certain that very inadequate views of those duties have been too often taken, both by those who conferred, and those who sustain the office; on that there is a manifest and loud call for an attempt to raise the standard of public sentiment in reference to the whole subject. *That we say so little of this office, compared with what we might do, and ought to do, does really appear to me one of the deepest deficiencies of our beloved Church. That a reform in this respect is desirable is to express but half the truth. It is necessary; it is vital.*[1] (emphasis mine)

Our study, therefore, must move into new territory and investigate the office of elder. The pastor who is planning for effectiveness must not be abandoned by the elders whose assistance he needs so critically!

SOME HISTORY

The purpose of this study does not demand a detailed analysis of the history of the office of Elder, but it is necessary to note that the Old Testament includes many references to the "elders of Israel" beginning already with Moses. Such elders were involved with Moses and Aaron in conveying the Word of God to the people, in representing the people before God on certain occasions, and in administering local government as well as national affairs. They achieved greater prominence during the Exile and after the Return and became associated with the judges in administering and executing justice. In the Maccabean period the title "elders of Israel" was used of the members of the Jewish Sanhedrin.

Their central role in the life of the church appears much more clearly in the New Testament. Paul sent Titus to Crete not only to "straighten out what was left unfinished..." but also to "...appoint elders in every town, as I directed you."[2] Throughout the New Testament three terms are used, variously translated as elder, pastor, bishop, or shepherd. It is generally and safely assumed that the terms

(EPISCOPOS, PRESBYTEROS, POIMAINOS) are synonyms and used interchangeably. For example, in I Peter 5:1,2 Peter uses all three interchangeably. We must understand, therefore, that in the early church there was not a clearly defined difference between the three. Indeed, the early church had not yet defined any of its offices very clearly. In I Timothy 5:17 we see the beginning of that process when Paul makes the distinction between elders "...who direct the affairs of the church..." and "...those whose work is preaching and teaching." The distinction originated there between ruling elders and teaching elders. The developing church, therefore, was led by a plurality of elders.

In the centuries that followed, however, this lay administered organization of the church gradually underwent a fundamental change. At some points the church focused on the work of elders and at other times on the work of deacons, but seemed unable to develop the ministry of both side by side. Sometimes the whole idea of lay leadership was rejected. During the first four centuries the diaconate gained an increasing role of importance, and the hierarchical structure which still characterizes the Roman Catholic Church came into being. The diaconate functioned as administrative assistants to the bishop and took on increasing liturgical responsibilities. After the fourth century the diaconate decreased in function and the eldership increased, eventually becoming an order of priests. Over several centuries, therefore, the office of elder as it functioned in the early church was lost, the distinction between ruling and teaching elders was no longer considered valid, and all attention and authority was focused on the hierarchical structure of priests and bishops.

REFORMATION REVISIONS

At the beginning of the sixteenth century the time was right for a change and a mighty religious movement that we have come to know as the Protestant Reformation swept across Europe. Its original purpose was not to start a new church but to cleanse the existing one from abuses and impurities. The faith of the New Testament church was re-examined and discovered anew. The full system of Christian Truth was once again set before the people. And a new examination of the organization and structure of the church was also a part of that effort and brought some fundamental changes.

John Calvin, one of the primary leaders of that movement, did much in his writing and preaching to carry the minds and hearts of the people back to the early Christian Church. Since the earliest Church was not carefully or clearly organized, Calvin focused his thoughts about structure on the church of the second century and taught that Christ has instituted four offices in the church: pastors who were to preach the Word of God; teachers who were to establish schools for the education of the young and old; ruling elders to maintain order and discipline; and deacons who were to administer charities for the poor.

Calvin was convinced that the elders of the church at Geneva should correspond closely to the "elders of the people" of the Old Testament. Consequently he clarified the policy for such a ruling body.

> These ruling elders were laymen, twelve in number, representing various parishes in the city and related to both the church and the civic government. They took an oath similar to that prescribed for the ministers. They met once each week with the pastors in a body known as the consistory to hear complaints against immoralities, or indecent language, or doctrinal errors, and any other matters that might corrupt the purity of the church and bring reproach to its good name.[3]

Churches in the Presbyterian and Reformed family have followed the lead of Calvin, though with some variations. Generally, however, they have been agreed on a number of principles concerning the government of the church: first, that leadership of the church should be vested in a plurality of leaders, second, that the plurality of leaders should be drawn from the local congregation, third, that there should be a distinction between ruling elders (who are responsible for the supervision of the church and its life) and teaching elders (who are responsible for preaching and teaching the Word of God), and finally, that there should be a distinction between lay leaders called elders who supervise the life of the church and deacons who are responsible for the ministry of mercy.

ELDER'S WORK

We have seen now that it is necessary for the church to benefit from the leadership of a plurality of elders. Even though the office of ruling elder and teaching elder was not clearly distinguished in the early church, and even though the tasks of elders are not precisely outlined in the New Testament, it is very well possible for us not only to reach the conclusion that Christ intended for elders to be present in every church, but also the general direction in which their responsibilities lie.

There are fourteen different words used in the New Testament in reference to the activity of elders. Some are more precise than others, but all together give us the clear impression that the functions of elders included four areas of responsibility.

The first area of responsibility is that of nurturing. In I Peter 5:1,2 the elders are exhorted by Peter, "...a fellow elder...", to "Be shepherds of God's flock that is under your care..." It is important that we understand Peter's willingness to link the concept of shepherd and elder so closely that they can be regarded as synonyms. A shepherd is preoccupied with feeding and caring for the flock and as such is intended to be a model for elders. A little later, in verse three, Peter sees the elders feeding and nurturing the sheep by setting their own wholesome example before them. In other words, their own lives are to function as a blueprint by which the members of the church may know how to structure their own lives. In Titus 1:9 Paul commands that elders must be willing and able to "...encourage others by sound doctrine...," that is, by feeding and nourishing them well on the truths of the Christian faith so they will be led to greater obedience and action. In I Thessalonians 5:12, Paul asks them to respect those who "...work hard among you..." and the word that Paul has selected (KOPIOUNTAS) is one that emphasizes the hard labor of concentrated effort to build someone up so that they might be productive and creative. Elders, therefore, must see the church as those who need to be nurtured well in the truth so that they will be obedient in their Christian service.

Secondly, they must defend the church. The body of Christ needs nurture in order to become productive; but must also be protected from enemies that aim to sabotage its existence. Therefore, the New Testament writers employ a number of terms that reflect the defensive stance that elders must take as they aim to protect the body of Christ. When Paul met with the elders from Ephesus at Miletus, he exhorted them to be faithful in their task with such terms. "Guard yourselves and all the flock of which the Holy Spirit has made you overseers."[4] The word he selected means to constantly hold the mind ready to detect and defend against the possible threats. Because false prophets, Pharisees, and other evil workers distort truth and destroy the church, the elders must stand guard. In exhorting them to be on their guard Paul selects a word that involves keeping wide awake and zealously alert to all possible threats. He warns them that the church will not have an easy road to travel in the world. Savage wolves will enter among the flock and even from within their number some will arise to sabotage the life of the church. The author of Hebrews employs the same term to describe leaders as those who "...keep watch over you as men who must give account."[5] Under those circumstances, elders who take a defensive stance are urgently needed.

A third area of responsibility is the provision of corrective care. Not all the difficulties of the church are potential, or outside the church. Some have already inflicted their damage and have led members of the church in the wrong direction. Correction, therefore, is another important ingredient of the task of faithful elders. To the Thessalonians, Paul describes the elders not only as those who work hard among them, being over them in the Lord, but also as those who "...admonish them."[6] The word he selects indicates a ministry of strong verbal warning and instruction about the dangers, weaknesses and failures that are present; a warning that arises out of a warm and loving spirit deeply concerned about their welfare. In Titus 1:9 Paul describes elders as those who must not only be able to encourage

others by sound doctrine but also to "...refute those who oppose it."
He is pointing to the activity of making an issue so clear that the
person being confronted will come under conviction. When Paul
describes the function of the God-breathed Scriptures in II Timothy
3:16, he selects this term again. So elders frequently find themselves
involved in the firm and loving correction that is needed in the body
of Christ.

The final responsibility of church elders is to provide directional
leadership. Another family of terms employed in the New Testament
lead us to picture elders as those who exercise their leadership by
setting the direction for the church and its members. In the passage
that we previously noted as the watershed for distinguishing the two
types of elders (I Timothy 5:17) Paul calls them those "...who direct
the affairs of the church..." he uses a participle with an adverb to give
us a picture of someone who serves as an excellent director, standing
at the head of a congregation, and leading it in the right direction.
When he speaks to the Thessalonians about "...those who are over
you in the Lord..."[7] he sketches a word picture of a superintendent
who manages them in such a way that they become productive. In his
listing of spiritual gifts Paul includes the gifts of "administration"[8] and
"leadership".[9] Both of these terms infer responsibilities concerning the
course of direction in which a group moves, whether it be a ship at sea
directed by its captain, or an organization that is directed by its leader.
Elders, therefore, are responsible for the direction that the church
takes.

It is not possible for us to know exactly how and in what way the
elders carried out these four dimensions of their task because the
terms in Scripture are very general. Nevertheless, it is very clear that
their role was an important one, and that the church cannot expect to
be as healthy and productive as Christ intends it to be unless faithful
elders are present. A companion publication, entitled *Now That You
Are An Elder,* provides a series of twelve "Study Guides For Church
Elders" that will be helpful to better understand this office and to
engage a group of elders in a study of the office to which they have

been called.

INVOLVED IN PREACHING

We cannot escape the conclusion therefore that a practice that is as much at the heart of the church as preaching must be a concern of elders who are faithful to their task. How can they ever be effective in nurturing, defending, correction and directing the church if they invest no time and effort in the development and maintenance of preaching? Yet one of the tragedies of the Christian church is that it has failed so consistently to develop this dimension of the office of elder. When the offices of ruling elder and teaching elder were distinguished from each other they seemed to move so far apart that both became weaker because of the distance from the other. I am convinced that the Spirit never intended it to be that way.

Research will indicate that historically the church has paid lip service to the joint efforts of elders and preachers. It is not difficult to find general statements such as: "The Elders share with the pastor the responsibility for the pulpit,"[10] and "An elder is an advisor of the pastor."[11] However more careful research will indicate that when such statements are made no one has in mind any efforts on the part of the elders in assisting the pastor in preparing for preaching by analyzing audience needs.

We are told that the elders must be sure that no person is allowed to enter the pulpit without their approval, or without the assurance of doctrinal purity. We are told the elders must be involved in examining and approving those who seek licensure to preach. We are told that the elders must serve as critics of preaching, evaluating it for doctrinal purity, effectiveness, and whether or not the preacher has been practicing the disciplines of careful sermon preparation.[12] In other words, the lay leaders in the office of elder have the right and responsibility to sit in judgment on the preaching **after** it has taken place.

Tragically, however, the church has never seen fit to emphasize that the elders must be involved in preaching **before** it takes place, in assisting the pastor in evaluating the needs of the congregation, in joining the pastor in conversations about the matters that must be addressed in preaching and the methods by which those matters can best be addressed. It sounds like the church encourages its elders to let the pastor plan for and carry out the preaching as he sees fit...and to let him know afterwards when it's not quite what the elders think it ought to be! So much potential assistance for the preacher and benefit for the congregation has been lost because the church has never seen that elders and preachers must work together in planning the preaching!

It is entirely reasonable to see that a plurality of elders (composed both of ruling and teaching elders) has greater wisdom and insight than one man. The biblical model verifies this. The Old Testament always speaks of a group of elders. In the New Testament Church, too, the emphasis is on a group. Never is the impression given that the leadership of a church is left in the hands of one person. How much richer the church would be then, and how much more effective its preaching, if pastor and elders would learn to work together in planning the preaching program for a local congregation.

Not only is there greater wisdom in a plurality of devoted minds, but also a joint analysis of the congregation and its needs can be so much more comprehensive and accurate. What an impossible task the pastor has when he is expected to understand and analyze the diverse needs and concerns of a modern congregation singlehandedly. Frankly, how inconsiderate of the eldership to expect that he will be able to satisfactorily carry out such a complex but critical task without assistance, but with the real possibility of their criticism if he doesn't do it satisfactorily.

The office of elder carries great potential for such significant contributions. Most churches in the Reformed and Presbyterian tradition have seen the role of elder as a pastoral role and have encouraged their elders to be involved in the lives of the members of the congregation. Paul S. Wright explains that a candidate for eldership is often asked, "Do you promise to study the peace, unity and purity of the church?"[13] P.Y. DeJong encourages the elders to be making regular visits to each family of the congregation so that they will "...know the spiritual condition of the flock over which the Lord has placed them."[14] Berghoef and De Koster insist that such family visiting "...provides ways to determine the precise needs of the congregation, and thus gives focus to preaching, deaconal assistance, teaching programs, and further attention to specific problems. Visiting takes the pulse and temperature of the body."[15] Richard De Ridder insists that "Elders must be pastors... This means more than attending consistory meetings or serving on church committees. The real business of the church is done outside the church building, when the leaders are with the flock — tending, feeding, caring for all members, young and old. Growing churches, spiritually strong churches, are those in which the leaders themselves know the members and are in close touch with them."[16] Yet nobody seems to take the next step and suggest that elders and the pastor are bound to confer regularly about the needs of the flock that must be addressed in the preaching of the Word.

The church today needs pastors who welcome the insight and advice that elders are able to give on the basis of their experience in life and their involvement in the lives of the members of the congregation. It certainly is true that the final responsibility for decisions about what to preach and how to preach it rest with the preacher himself. He is the man who ultimately stands accountable to God for what happens in the pulpit. But surely such a principle does not exclude the importance of receiving assistance and wise advice from a plurality of elders.

The church of today needs a body of elders who take their responsibility for preaching so seriously that they refuse to limit it merely to the right to criticize sermons that they believe may be off course, but include the responsibility to engage with the pastor in the evaluative and planning process that leads up to preaching. Who can better know the congregation than active elders who live with them and are a part of them? Who then is better able to provide insight and advice to the pastor than they?

At one elders meeting some time ago an incident happened that illustrates the point I am trying to make. Since I was in the process of planning my preaching for the coming year, I presented a list of eight possible series of messages that I was willing to consider preaching during that year. Of course, I felt more strongly about some than others. One of the series that I listed was a study of the book of Nehemiah, though I must confess I wasn't particularly inclined to such a study. I had included it to balance out the list of suggestions. In the discussion that evening, several of the elders pointed to the studies in Nehemiah as of particular interest to them personally and indicated that its message about the restoration of the people of God and Nehemiah's role of leadership would be very timely for our congregation. Their suggestions sparked more interest on my part, and eventually led to a series of eleven messages on Nehemiah that I personally found extremely fulfilling and to which the congregation responded with much more than normal appreciation. Had it not been for that discussion with the elders that series might never have been born!

The form that such discussions and evaluations take will certainly be different from one situation to another. Some may prefer to accomplish this by means of informal conversations periodically, although such loose arrangements generally prove less than satisfactory. Others may find that a group study using the "Study Guides for Church Elders," in the companion publication, *Now That You Are an Elder*, previously referred to will stimulate helpful insights and evaluations. Still others will set aside time on the agenda of each monthly meeting to allow opportunity to share insights about the congregation and its needs. In Appendix A is a tool that may also be helpful. There you will find a "Situational Analysis Form" that may be given to each elder to be completed on the basis of his awareness of the life of the congregation. Elders should be free to contribute any additional reflections that would be particularly helpful to the preacher. When the forms are tabulated, trends soon begin to appear.

The preacher considers all such insights and evaluations when he is ready to shape a season of preaching. Elder help will enable him to form a preliminary idea of which themes, studies, and passages will need to be treated. However, before he narrows the material down by final decisions, it would be wise for him to present the material to the elders once again for their reflections and suggestions. I usually take the opportunity to do that approximately twice a year. I present to my elders a list of possible sermon series for the next six to nine months. The list will include about twice the amount of material that I can hope to cover in that period. Their preferences, evaluations and suggestions are solicited and I find their guidance crucial in making the final selections.

1. Samuel Miller, *An Essay On The Warrant, Nature, and Duties Of The Office Of The Ruling Elder In The Presbyterian Church,* (Philadelphia: The Presbyterian Board of Publications, 1832), p. 5.

2. Titus 2:15.

3. Paul S. Wright, *The Duties Of The Ruling Elder,* (Philadelphia; The Westminster Press, 1957), p. 23-25.

4. Acts 20:28.

5. Hebrews 13:17.

6. I Thessalonians 5:12.

7. Ibid.

8. cf. I Corinthians 12:28.

9. cf. Romans 12:8.

10. Cleland Boyd Mc Afee, *The Ruling Elder,* (Philadelphia: Presbyterian Board of Christian Education, 1931), p. 57.

11. Ibid., p. 151.

12. Such statements are commonly found in the Book of Church Order, Ecclesiastical Manuals and Book of Church Government of many denominations.

13. Paul S. Wright, *The Duties Of The Ruling Elder,* (Philadelphia: The Westminster Press, 1957), p. 52.

14. Peter Y. De Jong, *Taking Heed To The Flock,* (Grand Rapids: Baker Book House, 1948), p. 65.

15. Gerald Berghoef and Lester De Koster, *The Elders Handbook,* (Grand Rapids: Christian's Library Press, 1979), p. 92.

16. Richard R. De Ridder, *In His Service: Special Offices Of The Church (4),* (Grand Rapids: CRC Publications, 1986), p. 10.

CHAPTER SEVEN

The Balanced Pulpit

O ur journey has taken us to a critical juncture. The Discipline of
Rhetoric shows that audience analysis is crucial for effective
communication, including preaching. In addition, both the
Gospels and the Epistles illustrate the skill of audience adaptation in
messages that communicate well. We have pointed toward the elders
of the church as necessary assistants in the process.

If these directives are followed the preacher will have a wealth of
information and impressions available to him. He must now begin to
pull all of that together in order to focus it on an appropriate pulpit
ministry.

As he does so there is another consideration—balance in preaching.
At the end of a pulpit season, or at the end of five years, or ten, he
must be able to look back and see that he has presented a balanced diet
to the people of God. Balance in the pulpit is as important as balance
in nutrition if the cause of spiritual health is to be served well.

One of my wife's hobbies is nutrition. For years she has been
studying the matter and is thoroughly convinced that it's the key to
good health. One word that is very prominent in her nutritional vocabulary is "balance". I hear her speaking about a good balance between
breakfast, lunch and supper. She insists on a healthy balance between

carbohydrates, proteins and fats. She'll say to me, "you've really had enough of that this week, you should balance it out with some of this…" Frankly, I could eat all-American hamburgers every night of the week, but she tells me I need balanced meals. So our family has good confidence knowing that the design of our nutrition is in her hands. It makes sense when she tells us that developing and maintaining good health requires such balance.

Preachers, who are responsible for designing the pulpit diet of the church could stand to learn some lessons from her. The same principles are true—good growth requires proper nourishment, and proper nourishment requires a healthy nutritional balance. The development and maintenance of good spiritual health requires a spiritually balanced diet.

But that's not so easy to plan; and as we have seen there are some great dangers inherent in leaving all such choices to the preacher alone. The preacher is subject to the insidious temptation to set his own agenda for the pulpit. It's always easier for us to concentrate on our own interests while avoiding those matters that might be more difficult or controversial. The bottom line is that if the entire pulpit diet is left to the discretion of the preacher alone it could become very unbalanced. Reflect on what happened in some of these recent settings:

> —I visited some friends at Thanksgiving and while worshiping with them discovered their pastor was preaching a series of messages from Jeremiah. A year later I stopped in again and learned that he was "still stuck in Jeremiah" and they were becoming very weary of it.
> —"Our pastor is always dealing with prophecy," a friend said. "He is far more interested in reading all the little indicators of the signs of the times than helping me with some of my personal struggles."
> —A frustrated man told me, "All we get around here is that heavy doctrinal stuff week after week, until I feel like my head is twice its size and my heart is shrinking."
> —Another said, "We get so much milk and such little meat in our church that I feel I ought to take my head off and put it under the seat. It's just not needed."

What is wrong in each of these situations? Concerns that are very appropriate are overdone, or at least perceived as overdone, and an unhealthy imbalance has resulted. Each pastor was dealing with very good concerns (Jeremiah is a good book; prophecy is important; doctrine must be taught; milk is necessary; confronting error is crucial) but failed to hold his interests in balance with other concerns. My garden isn't all beans; we've made room for lettuce, peppers, and tomatoes. My wife won't let me have a diet of all hamburgers; she insists on salads, fish, vegetables, etc. Of course!

One of the reasons why it's hard to maintain a balanced pulpit diet is that it's so hard to define just what balance is. The material my wife has studied on nutrition points to guidelines that would include about 60% complex carbohydrates, 20% protein, and 20% fat in our diet. And she has charts and tables in books to help her carefully follow such guidelines. Are there any such simple tools for the preacher? Unfortunately not! That is precisely the problem of the preacher.

I have done a lot of searching and have found very little helpful material for the preacher. I have scoured homiletical textbooks and journal articles. I have interviewed several homiletical professors as well. And, while I know that my search has not been exhaustive, frankly, I've gained very little concrete information—only a few suggestions that involve bare glimpses of the direction in which we'll have to go.

Nor could I get a lot of help from the Scriptures which never seem to address the matter carefully. I understand why that is so. The writers of Scripture never have in view a preacher who has been engaged in a sustained pulpit ministry to the same congregation over a long period of time. I will soon have preached nearly 1000 sermons in my present pulpit. The Apostles moved on after a little while in each town. Paul's three-year stay in Ephesus seems to be the maximum for him. He seems to come close to some guidelines in Acts 20:27 when he explains to the Elders of Ephesus that he did not hesitate to "...proclaim to you the whole will of God." Yet there are no details, no specifics, no guidelines about what we have to preach to be satisfied that we're preaching the "whole will of God." I wish he had given some. I would love to sit down with Paul and ask him some of my questions about it all.

I also raised the question about how to define balance in one of the meetings of our Board of Elders some time ago. After explaining my concern to them, and presenting some analysis of the passages and subjects I had treated in my preaching in recent years, I asked the big question: "Just what does it take for preaching to be balanced, as you think of it?" A good discussion ensued as they wrestled with the question. They made some very helpful suggestions. "Balance means remembering all the age groups of the congregation, and the concerns that are unique to each," one said. Another pointed out that a sermon needs internal balance so that at various points in the same sermon an awareness of all ages and their needs is evident. Still another said, "You can be confident you have balance in your preaching when you look back over a year of preaching and see that you've been sensitive to all the diverse needs that are in this church. Some of us need encouragement, some of us need to be disturbed, and some of us need to be called to Christ." Another Elder insisted that we must clarify our definition of preaching first. He explained that he believes preaching must present the Word of God for the purpose of (1) building faith, (2) giving knowledge, (3) calling people to Jesus Christ, and (4) equipping them for service. "When you work at fulfilling those four tasks," he said, "you've got a pretty good balance."

So I have attempted to formulate some criteria by which we can better understand the balance we need. I present these for your consideration. As I have tried to define balance, it has been helpful for me to approach the matter from six different directions.

CANONICAL BALANCE

It is important to make the canon of Scripture one of the criteria. Plenary inspiration means that all of Scripture from Genesis to Revelation is inspired of God, authoritative, and therefore legitimate material for preaching. Progressive revelation means that you expect God's revelation to take on greater clarity as you move from the

beginnings of the Scripture to the latter books. But all of it has authority, and all must be represented. Yet it certainly is true that not all passages of Scriptures have equal homiletical value. It is entirely
reasonable that I treat the six chapters of Ephesians with greater concentration than the fifty-two chapters of Jeremiah, for example.

I remember that one of my Seminary Professors had indicated to us
once that a good rule of thumb was to preach a third of the time from
the Old Testament, another third of the time from the Gospels, and the
final third of the time from the remainder of the New Testament. So I
set to work evaluating the last ten years of my preaching. I discovered
that 32% of my time was spent in the Old Testament; 26% of it was
spent in the Gospels; and 42% was spent in the reminder of the New
Testament. I began to see a trend in my preaching selections. It is perhaps easier for me to select didactic passages than any other. I must be
careful of that; it could tilt the scale too far one way.

Then I considered the various types of literature that are included in
the Scriptures. I was taught that the richness of the Scriptures is due,
in part, to the valuable literary diversity. Some of the books are historical, some are wisdom literature, others prophecy, some biography, and
others are doctrinal material. I wondered how my preaching would be
distributed across those five categories, so I tabulated the same ten
years of preaching according to the passages that I had treated and was
very surprised at what I found.

24% was from historical books

15% was from wisdom literature

10% was from prophetic books

30% was from biographical books

21% was from doctrinal books.

I began to see trends, and weaknesses. It was understandable that such
a concentration was found in the historical and biographical books
because God's mighty acts are performed in history, and we see his
works best in the lives of people and nations. However, was I negli-
gent in side-stepping wisdom literature and prophetic books? I exam-
ined my pattern of devotional studies, and discovered the same trend

in the books of the Bible that I select for my devotional reading. I gained a new appreciation for the importance of doing justice to the full range of the canon of Scripture.

CONFESSIONAL BALANCE

In the tradition of our denomination, the congregation worships twice each Sunday, morning and evening, with a different sermon at each service. In addition, our Church Order requires that, "At one of the services each Lord's Day, the minister shall ordinarily preach the Word as summarized by the Heidelberg Catechism..."

I am convinced there are some real advantages to such a practice. In a day when so many Christians are not well grounded in the basic truths of the Christian faith, such a steady diet of confessional preaching will give just what they need. It's also good discipline for the preacher because it forces him to deal with passages and truths that he might otherwise ignore. It also provides a good sense of historical identity because we sense that Christians of other generations have professed the same faith, struggled with the same concerns, and lived by the same hope.

Besides, there is a large matter of convenience built into such a system; as the preacher plans his pulpit work for the season, the schedule for one of those services is pretty well decided for him.

But there are some significant disadvantages as well. Preaching confessionally can be very challenging, especially if you are determined to make it fresh, relevant and interesting. It runs the risk of weighing the preaching diet heavily in the direction of didactic and doctrinal material, thus creating its own imbalance. It certainly can become a test for the pastor who remains in the same congregation for more than 5 or 6 years.Can I cover the same material again and remain fresh? Should I just rely on the sermon material I used last time? For the preacher prone to seek out shortcuts the traps are all too obvious. For the congregation tempted to be impatient with doctrinal preaching, the load will quickly become heavy.

How can the preacher preserve the balance of capitalizing on the

advantages of confessional preaching while compensating for its disadvantages? I have wrestled hard with that question and have devised
a plan for myself that retains the conviction that confessional preaching is essential to healthy nurture for the congregation, yet packages it
with sufficient balance to avoid some of its stiffest hazards.

This plan allows for two years to cover the fifty-two Lord's Days of
the Heidelberg Catechism. That provides enough elbow room in the
preaching schedule to allow breaks for Lent, Advent, and at other
times. However, since our denomination holds to two other major
Confessions (The Belgic Confession of Faith and the Canons of Dort)
as well as a Contemporary Testimony ("Our World Belongs To God"),
I have chosen, with the agreement of our Board of Elders, to include a
study of those Confessions alternately with the Catechism. Over a ten
year period of time, therefore, my schedule of Confessional Preaching
will look something like this:

Heidelberg Catechism (two years)
The Canons of Dort (one-half year)
Heidelberg Catechism (two years)
Belgic Confession of Faith (one year)
Heidelberg Catechism (two years)
The Contemporary Testimony (one year)
Heidelberg Catechism (two years)

With such a pattern I can uphold the conviction that Confessional
Preaching is necessary for a maturing faith. I can also provide a balance even in Confessional Preaching since some historic Christian
doctrines are dealt with more carefully in one confession than in
another. I am assured therefore that over a period of time I have presented to the congregation, on a regular basis, a balanced diet of the
historic Christian Faith.

TELIC BALANCE

Jay Adams, in *Preaching With Purpose,* makes the claim, "There
are few deficiencies in preaching quite so disastrous in their effect as
the all-too-frequently occurring failure to determine the *telos* (or pur-

pose) of a preaching portion."[1] The *telos* is the original intent that the Holy Spirit had when he inspired a particular portion of Scripture.

If the Spirit always had a *telos*/purpose/intent in mind while doing the work of inspiration, then surely the preacher must have an equally clear idea of that as he aims to communicate the inspired Scriptures to his hearers today. The crucial question for the preacher then is, "what is the purpose of this sermon that I am to preach on Sunday?"

It's not always so simple to answer a question like that, and we need to wrestle with it in regards to each message. We need also live with an awareness that preaching as a whole has multiple purposes. I mentioned previously the Elders Meeting in which one of the men pointed to four purposes of preaching—to build faith, give knowledge, call people too Christ, and equip them to service.

Jay Adams, in the book just mentioned, prefers to speak of two kinds of preaching in terms of its basic purpose. Evangelistic Preaching has as its purpose the announcement of God's good news to people so that they will come to faith in Jesus Christ. Edificational Preaching has as its purpose the nurture and teaching of the believer so that he will be built up in the faith and equipped for obedient service.[2]

I remember a Seminary Professor who once said you can reduce all the various purposes of preaching to this—to comfort the afflicted, and to afflict the comfortable!

Paul, in II Timothy 3:16,17, points to the fourfold purpose of Scripture (and therefore preaching) that will thoroughly equip the man of God for every good work through (1) teaching, (2) rebuking, (3) correcting, and (4) training in righteousness.

Dr. Karl Menninger, in *Whatever Became Of Sin?* points to his understanding of the purpose of preaching when he says that the person in the pulpit has "...an unparalleled opportunity to lighten burdens, interrupt and redirect circular thinking, relieve the pressure of guilt feelings and their self-punishment, and inspire individual and social improvement."

It is understandable that preaching has multiple purposes because the audience before the preacher ordinarily is an audience with widely varying spiritual states, and even more diverse personal experiences. In *The Art of Preaching,* William Perkins told us many years ago to think of six categories of hearers, three of them converted and three of them unconverted. Among the converted, there are those who are young children and need to be built up, those who are under temptation and trouble and need to be supported, and those who are mature and need to advance in the faith. Among the unconverted, there are those who are spiritually indifferent and need arousing, those who are spiritually conceited and need humbling, and those who are humbled, anxious and seeking, and need to be led into the kingdom of God.

With such a diversity before him, and such broad purposes for preaching, the preacher must remain self-critical of the purposes of his preaching. He must be engaged in constant review of what he is trying to do and what his congregation needs. Some need to be convicted of their sin and brought to salvation; others need comfort in a time of doubt and crisis. Some need to be exposed for their wanderings; others need to be grounded better in the basics of the faith. Some need to be confronted about their complacency, and still others need to be challenged to more committed service. The list could go on.

There are no neat and easy formulas to use for retaining such a balance. Constant analysis is required, and the assistance of spiritually alert Elders in touch with the needs of the congregation will be a precious ally of the preacher who is concerned about telic balance.

CHURCH-YEAR BALANCE

A significant rhythm is built into our ecclesiastical year and the experience of that rhythm must be a part of preaching balance. During Old Testament times the Israelites celebrated a year that was marked off by certain festivals and feasts through which they rhythmically observed the great acts of God. In New Testament times, when God has renewed his covenant through Jesus Christ, the Christian Church is still called to rhythmically celebrate the great acts of God.

So in the experience of Christians today the eager anticipation of Advent gives way to the celebration of the incarnation at Christmas.

The incarnation lays the foundation for the ministry of Jesus which ushers in the time of Lent, then the triumph of Easter, the Ascension of Christ, and the coming of the Spirit at Pentecost. Six times of festival, therefore, dominate the spirit and temperament of the ecclesiastical year—Christmas, Palm Sunday, Good Friday, Easter, Ascension Day, and Pentecost. The great themes of God's redemptive work are always portrayed on these six pages of the calendar.

The preacher who is interested in pulpit balance must take this ecclesiastical calendar into consideration in planning his season of pulpit work. A program of preaching, no matter how excellent in other respects, that ignores these events is guilty of inexcusable deficiencies.

For that reason, many have chosen to follow the *Common Lectionary* in their preaching. Though I do not follow it directly, I have spoken to those who have and find them very eager to speak its praises. The Lectionary provides a planned schedule for preaching that is built around these great Christian festivals and is constructed for three years. It presents a balanced treatment of Old Testament and New Testament as well as the Christological events of God's redemptive plan. For each Sunday, on a three year cycle, four Scripture lessons are presented from both the Old and New Testaments. Those who plan their preaching accordingly can be assured that they will receive healthy assistance in helping them avoid overemphasizing or neglecting certain themes.

Andrew Blackwood, a homiletician at Princeton Seminary of another generation, takes a similar but slightly different approach in his *Planning a Year's Pulpit Work*.[3] He suggests that our pulpit season from September to Christmas should be characterized by "undergirding" and should aim to reveal God and His ways through Bible History and should preach Christian doctrine. From Christmas to Easter we must aim for "recruiting" and must proclaim the beauty of the Gospel and the message of the Cross. From Easter to Pentecost our aim must be "instructing" in which we present the risen Lord and preach Bible Ethics. Finally, from Pentecost to September our aim should be "heartening" and we must meet the life situations of the hearers.

So the preacher who engages in the balancing act will always have his eye on the church calendar.

ISSUE BALANCE

I am continually impressed, and frequently frightened, with the great diversity of need in the audience that sits before me each Sunday. I look them over while the offering is being taken and I'm preparing to lead them in prayer, and I wonder how I can ever get in touch with all their needs. "They are too many, and too different, Lord!" I want to cry out. I see a young lady who comes every month with a new boyfriend; a father who feels guilty over some dishonesty at work; a young couple with wounds of misunderstanding; a lonely widow; grieving parents of a rebellious son; a young father who found a tumor; another who is angry about the heavy blows of life; a family with great joy that needs to be expressed; another couple just starting a family; a father who dreads approaching retirement...and the list goes on.

Such an awareness points to the importance of "Situational Preaching" as set forth in Chapter #2. The preacher must possess ears that are ready to pick up signals from others about trends and patterns in the lives of his hearers. He must be a pastor who is in touch with the world of his parishioners. He must feel their pulse and breathe their concerns. He also must have the full assistance of alert and observant elders who realize this is part of their task. So the preacher who aims for an "issue balance" in his preaching has a formidable task. He will have to be engaged in a regular effort to study and discern the pressing needs in the lives of his listeners. He must be praying not only that the Spirit of God will open his mind to understand what the Word is saying, but also that the Spirit will open his mind to discern what his parishioners are experiencing.

As I became increasingly aware of this, I spent time analyzing my preaching of the past ten years. As I indicated previously, nearly half of that preaching was confessional in character. The other half of it was usually structured around series of messages that vary from 3-10 sermons each. My analysis revealed to me that my preaching was spread rather evenly across seven categories of content:

> Series for the Church Year (Advent, Lent, etc.)
> Direct Biblical Studies (a book or chapter of the Bible)
> Biographical Studies (a person from the Scriptures)
> Issues of the Christian Life (moral and ethical issues)
> Issues of Christian Belief (various positions of doctrine)
> Life and Mission of the Church (its identity and work)
> Christian Renewal (the life of faith in a changing world)

Each preacher must consciously and self-critically, therefore, aim for a balance in the issues that preaching addresses.

METHODOLOGY BALANCE

My parishioners worship a lot. We worship twice every Sunday. Approximately 75% of our members are present every Sunday morning; 65% of them are present again at night. Both services are preaching services. Therefore the average parishioner hears nearly 75-80 sermons per year and some hear much more than that.

I'm very grateful for that kind of faithfulness and loyalty. However, it also makes preaching to them very challenging. It takes a lot of effort to avoid the rut of "sameness." Someone has said that the only difference between a rut and a grave is how long you stay in it! To retain a healthy interest level in preaching requires variation in method, as well as the other factors we've considered. To come to church regularly expecting the same method of presentation removes a good bit of interest. Interesting preaching may not always be so predictable. An unwholesome predictability descends on a congregation like a pall and keen communication is hurt.

Our culture is built on variety. Art, music, architecture, and literature all attest to that fact. Hardly anything stays the same for two consecutive appearances. Yet, sadly, preaching often does. We use the same method, follow the same pattern, think in the same structures, outline in the same way...unless, of course, we are willing to expend the extra energy to step outside of our comfortable and ordinary routine and push the boundaries back to make room for some variation.

Fred Craddock, in *Preaching,* says "No form is so good that it does not eventually become wearisome to both listener and speaker."[4] Harold Freeman, in *Variety in Biblical Preaching*, encourages us to develop alternate methods to our usual ones.[5] Dramatic monologues, he says, have new power to capture attention. A dialogic message can make hearers face the truth in new ways. A narrative message utilizing the art of story-telling can reach previously unreached ears. A segmented message may use several different methods of communication. Other means can also be employed to augment the verbal message. He makes one think about the prophets who used not only a verbal discourse but also a torn robe, a smear of ashes, a basket of summer fruit, a plumb-line, and even a cistern to get the same message across in more communicative ways. The Master Communicator presented a verbal monologue, used a stirring story, a little child, and miracles to enhance his communicative effectiveness.

So I've made some attempts along that line, always trying to take into consideration the limitations of my own personal abilities and the limitations of what my parishioners would accept. (Actually **inappropriate** variation sabotages instead of enhances communication.) In some series I will work expositorily through a book or chapter a few verses at a time. In another series I'll portray the dynamics of the personal life of one of the Biblical characters. At another time I'll treat a number of pressing moral/ethical issues in a problem-solving manner. I have worked my way through the life of Joseph, in Genesis 37-50, in first-person narrative style. I've dealt with the great theme of salvation by grace in the form of my life story. I presented my thoughts about Christian Education in a "Why My Children Are in Christian School" method.

The possibilities are many. They are limited only by our own willingness to work hard at being creative, and our understanding of what methods will be acceptable in our community.

Seeking balance in preaching is no easy matter. We must keep more than one isolated criteria in mind. I began my thinking about the matter with the assumption it would be easy to develop several very simple guidelines, but since life just doesn't allow itself to be reduced to

simple guidelines, neither does preaching. Yet the matter of communicating well is so crucial we may never ignore the issue, nor give up on
the work.

Balance begs for the preacher to be self-critical, not merely to
engage in Monday morning quarterbacking about the day before. He
must always be reviewing and analyzing each season before another
one is planned.

It also begs the preacher to plan ahead. The preacher who works
and plans only from Monday to Sunday is subject to the fickle ploys
of whim. Only when he plans a whole season of preaching at a time is
he able to refine his methods and keep an eye on his balance.

It begs church Elders to refuse to leave the preacher alone with this
task. The issue is too big to lay in the lap of one person. To be sure, the
final decision about what to preach and what to say in that preaching
belongs to the preacher who is personally accountable to God.
However, he cannot do that effectively without elders who assist him in
pointing out trends and needs that require the attention of preaching.

In his *Preaching In A Scientific Age,* Dr. A.C. Craig of Glasgow
University said that about a year or so after he was ordained to the
ministry he happened to meet Principal Alexander Martin one day in
Edinburgh. Martin greeted him with the question, "well, how's the
preaching going?" When Craig said he was finding it difficult, Martin
expressed no surprise. Craig goes on to say that, if pressed for an
amplification of this, Dr. Martin would probably have gone on to say
something to this effect; "Young man, do not imagine that you will
ever master the glamorous, elusive art of preaching. If you have the
authentic call to it, it will enslave you, enchant you, tease you, con-
found you all your days: and in the end you will have to say, 'I have
not attained, I only press toward the mark of this high calling'."[6]

1. Jay E. Adams, *Preaching With Purpose,* (Grand Rapids: Baker Book House,
1982), p. 27.

2. Ibid., p. 6.

3. cf. Andrew Blackwood, *Planning A Year's Pulpit Work,* (Nashville: Abingdon-
Cokesbury Press, 1942).

4. Fred B. Craddock, *Preaching,* (Nashville: Abingdon Press, 1985), p. 177.

5. cf. Harold Freeman, *Variety In Biblical Preaching,* (Waco: Word Books, 1987).

6. Archibald C. Craig, *Preaching In A Scientific Age,* (New York: Scribner's Sons, 1954), p. 7, 8.

CHAPTER EIGHT

Planning A Pulpit Season

A cartoon in one of the early issues of *Leadership* poignantly portrayed the panic pastors frequently experience. The pastor sat at his desk, books piled high, eyes wide with fright, head resting wearily on both hands. Behind him was a bigger than life wall calendar for the month all neatly sectioned off in its appropriate boxes. However, this calendar was different. It was "The Preacher's Calendar" and the difference is that every other column was labelled "Sunday" while the alternate ones were labelled "Monday-Saturday".

I remember that feeling from my first pastorate all too well! Every other day seemed like Sunday. I couldn't imagine why they rolled around so fast with their demand for more sermons. I usually tried to take Monday as my day off but the attempted relaxation of Monday was always overshadowed by the approaching panic of Tuesday morning—"what am I going to preach on this week?" The panic increased mathematically if such uncertainty carried into Wednesday and even Thursday!

Throughout the course of my ministry I have found a solution that delivered me from such unpleasantries. It not only removed panic, but also made sermon writing and preaching so much more fascinating and rewarding. I found this solution when I began to plan ahead in my preaching, eventually developing a system by which I would plan an entire pulpit season (September through August) before it began.

I know that my personal make-up enters into my convictions about the matter. I don't enjoy working under last-minute pressure, nor am I convinced that I do my best work under those circumstances. Maybe others do, though I'm willing to question that. I'm convinced that sermon preparation goes better, preaching will be of better quality, the whole experience will be much more satisfying for the preacher, and others who share Sunday worship responsibilities will be grateful when the preacher plans in advance.

I didn't arrive at this plan by surprise. It didn't suddenly come to me like a flash out of the blue. I learned it from others and my firm commitment to this method has been molded by a number of central convictions.

I am convinced that there are benefits for high quality preaching that can be achieved in no other way than through advanced planning. I will point to some of those benefits later, but it must be understood that sermon writing done at the last minute, under the pressure of inadequate time, with little forethought, cannot be expected to produce a high quality product.

That consideration becomes all the more important when I remember that the calling to stand in the pulpit with the awesome responsibility of bringing the Word of God to waiting worshipers is a task that demands our best, not our leftovers. It is a task so high and noble that it requires the highest priority on our list of duties. Haphazard planning is beneath the dignity of a preaching ministry.

In addition, the message that I am communicating to my congregation by advanced planning (and it does become obvious over a period of time) is one that tells them I take preaching seriously and they should too.

Courtesy toward the other worship leaders is another important consideration. Both I and the congregation expect that organists, choir directors, etc. give us excellent leadership. But how can I expect them to do that, if it becomes clear that I don't? The preacher is the pacesetter in determining how much careful thought is given to the life of worship of the congregation.

OUTSTANDING BENEFITS

Convictions like that made me very open to the idea of advanced planning, but once I actually began it I discovered the benefits were so outstanding that I wondered why I hadn't initiated such a plan long before. I guess we are always motivated by those matters that benefit us personally, and I surely discovered that planning helped me.

That sense of panic early in the week became one of the most distasteful parts of the ministry for me. "What will I preach about this week...and how?..." tied my stomach in knots. Then I began projecting even farther ahead. Will I still be doing this ten years from now and feeling the same way about it? I began to seriously face the possibility of running dry, being able to come up with nothing except what I had already done over and over. Over the horizon of my ministry I could see a defeated and weary pulpiteer approaching with a plaintive cry "I don't know what to preach about anymore!"

No more! My right hand drawer has a file in it labelled "Hopper For Preaching" and it's bulging because I keep tossing in the ideas, passages, themes, and series that I am eager to get at some day. My problem now is that there aren't enough sermons in the year to keep up with ideas that are incubating in my hopper (and enough time to research and write them all!). I am ever so glad to be past panic.

I've also discovered that advanced planning helps me to gain a much broader view of my preaching. I'm not preoccupied with the Sunday immediately before me, but I have an overall picture of the whole season. That puts me in a better position to achieve a balanced pulpit diet and to avoid pushing my own pet peeves! Maintaining such a balanced diet requires an over-all view. I couldn't do that when I lived from week to week, but when I sketch out a whole season at a time I can. Every preacher must be able to look back at five or ten years of his pulpit ministry and be pleased that he has fed his flock with a nutritiously balanced diet of the great truths of the Word.

Preaching ideas generally need a while to incubate before they are ready for sermons. None of us would deny that preaching is a very difficult task. Maybe we're not really sure that we've caught the core thought of our passage and it needs some more exegesis; or maybe we're not sure that we have clarified exactly what it means for our hearers today; or how to apply it. Maybe we can't be sure that we have found the best and most effective way to communicate it to the congregation. Yet Sunday keeps rolling down the tracks like an approaching locomotive that cannot be slowed. Many of our messages would be much clearer in focus, more appropriate in application, and more effectively communicated if they could incubate for a number of weeks.

I told my congregation that I would honor their requests for sermons during the Sunday evenings of a recent summer. Out of the many requests that came in, one suggested that I preach on II Kings 2:23-25, and address the matter of respect for our leaders on the basis of Elisha's encounter with the jeering youths and the quick judgment of God on them. I knew that was one request that I had to honor. I had a great deal of uncertainty about how to approach that passage without running the risk of making it say things that it didn't intend to say. All summer I collected notes and scribblings for that sermon. The file folder held them all for me. Finally, by the time the week for writing that sermon rolled around I felt pregnant with a message—much in contrast to my initial apprehensions.

Advanced planning also enables me to give much more direction to my personal study. All of us preachers know that we should study, but we all also feel the intense pressure of other responsibilities. Late planning, or no planning, therefore, usually eliminates much serious study on a passage. We have to "go with what we've got on hand" because deadlines are approaching. Sometimes that's safe; often it's terribly dangerous. Advanced planning helps us anticipate the subjects we ought to be studying, and gives us the opportunity to plan our personal reading diet to complement our preaching schedule.

Gordon MacDonald prefers to make a distinction between "offensive studying" and "defensive studying". While defensive studying is done under the pressure of an approaching deadline, offensive studying is that general, much broader studying that is done for general learning. If we plan only from week to week, we can't really do much more than defensive studying. Advanced planning, however, gives us the opportunity to be engaged in much more offensive studying. In an interview on *Preaching Today,* MacDonald explained that as he developed maturity and focus in his ministry, he found the proportion between offensive and defensive studying changing significantly. He claimed that early in his ministry the proportion was 90% defensive of 10% offensive, but later it became approximately 70% defensive and 30% offensive.

There is still another benefit of advanced planning. It helps us collect better illustrative material. No one can overestimate the power of appropriate illustrations properly placed. Many excellent sermons have never been lifted off the ground because there were no illustrations to lift them. We all know the frustration of discovering the perfect illustration—three days after we've preached the sermon in which we needed it. So on the shelf behind me there is a file folder for the sermons that I'll be preaching during the next six months (incubators). I try to keep them all in mind and when an appropriate illustration comes to my attention I can drop it in that folder and I know that I'll have more than I need when that sermon has to be written.

That also solves another problem. I'm always collecting illustrations, quotes, facts, and little stories. They turn up in my personal conversations, my experiences, and my reading. I put them all on 3x5 cards. Then what? I used to let them sit in a little pile on my desk for awhile to see if a place for them could be found, and then after a few weeks I would file them in my topical file drawer—and many of them will probably stay there until I retire. Now, before they get assigned to the file drawer, they are matched up with the proper incubator and I'm convinced that my use of good illustrative material has increased significantly.

The benefits of advanced planning for preaching are so outstanding that I'll never go back to living week by week.

PRAYER ANALYSIS

Some are skeptical of advanced planning because it sounds like it will only add more work to a schedule that is already too full. I have found just the opposite. Work becomes more efficient and time is used to greater advantage, provided that the proper method of advanced planning is found. Poor methods could indeed multiply work instead of decrease it, but the proper methods actually diminish our work by allowing for greater efficiency.

The most important stage is the preparatory period of gathering information and impressions even before specific planning begins. I know that preachers have often debated about how we can best be open to the leading of the Holy Spirit in our pulpit ministry. Some have insisted that the Spirit leads us best in the spontaneity of the moment. Surely we've all experienced those times when a message took an unanticipated and unplanned turn while it was being delivered to address some special need. We've been heartened to experience the Spirit's leading under those circumstances. Some have wanted to go farther and insist that minimal or no preparation is best so the Spirit can have free reign. Most of us, however, understand the Spirit to be very present in all our processes of research, exegesis, writing, and assimilation as well as in the actual delivery of the sermon.

We must broaden our awareness of the direction of the Spirit to include all our preparation and planning efforts, even those a year ahead of time. I am confident that there are needs that will exist in this congregation six months and a year from now that preaching must address, and since I cannot now be aware of those, the Spirit takes them all into consideration in directing my planning. The umbrella of the Spirit's direction is so big that all my preparation and planning fits under it.

So when planning for a new season begins it must be surrounded with fervent prayer. The summer months are my months for planning because they usually involve a somewhat slower pace. Our Elders should be informed that such planning will soon be underway and their prayers are needed. The congregation should be informed of that as well, perhaps by a bulletin or newsletter explanation. Other staff members should be drawn into the prayers for pulpit planning. Daily I pray for wisdom from the Spirit for I know that all my personal planning will likely go in the wrong direction if it doesn't remain under the tutelage of the Spirit.

However, all the prayer in the world will not obviate the need for a careful analysis of the needs of the congregation that must be addressed in preaching. While the preacher must know the Word to proclaim it, he must also know the world of his listeners so he can proclaim it appropriately and effectively. Surveys that I have conducted indicate that most pastors gather material about the needs of their parishioners through pastoral calling, pastoral counseling, informal associations with their parishioners, wide reading, and discussions with the elders of the Church.

My own process usually involves four steps. First I will review my own notes about matters that need to be addressed and questions that need to be answered as I have accumulated them in my "Hopper For Preaching". In late spring or early summer I have distributed an insert in the weekly bulletin inviting all parishioners to make any comments or suggestions they would like concerning "matters that you believe should be addressed, or passages that need to be taught, in preaching during the next year." I study these comments carefully and try to detect trends in them. During the summer my Elders are given a "Situational Analysis Form" (cf. Appendix A) which they each complete. I study those carefully too. At the next Elders meeting I usually present to them a list of the series of messages that I am considering for the coming year with a brief explanation of the material these series will cover. I present about twice the number that is needed and explain to them that they are to participate with me in narrowing down the selections. Each Elder makes his selections, in writing, and I tabulate those results.

By this time I have accumulated a great deal of information and impressions, all of which has been bathed in prayer.

CHARTING IT

It's time now to approach the task of planning in earnest. To have accumulated a lot of information is only the beginning. Conclusions and plans must be distilled from it.

Some pastors I have spoken to prefer to set aside an entire week or two in August to chart out the coming year. I usually spread my planning through the month of August and reduce my pastoral work to allow time for it. In either case, the work can be best done away from the church where distractions and interruptions can be minimized. Some go to a retreat place, I often do it in a neighboring college library, but I often dream of a quiet cabin by the water for that.

The process at this point requires that a skeleton outline for the entire year be charted out. I usually work from September through the following August because that coincides with the church year. At this point my process involves six steps.

1. I chart out on paper the 52 Sundays from September through August. Since we worship twice each Sunday and both services require a different sermon, I use a standard sheet of paper with three columns: for the date, the morning service, and the evening service. It looks like this:

date	a.m. service	p.m. service
Sept. 6		
Sept. 13		
Sept. 20		
Sept. 27		
Oct. 4, etc.		

2. Then I work my way through the entire calendar and fill in the previously designated events of an ecclesiastical nature that must be observed. The season of Advent and Lent must be noted on the calendar. Our celebration of Thanksgiving, Christmas, Good Friday, Easter, Ascension Day, Pentecost, etc. must be included. The specific purpose

of each event dictates the content.

3. There are also events of a more local nature that must be included. On certain Sundays we will be celebrating Communion so I mark those in. Reformation Day, Mother's Day, Father's Day, and Respect Human Life Sunday will be marked in. In January we have two weeks of Mission Emphasis and Sundays must be reserved for that. Another service is set aside for the ordination of new office bearers. In each case I make note of the content.

4. Then I mark out those times when I plan to be away. Vacation time, free services, and other commitments take me out of town. This information is noted by the Worship Committee so they can arrange pulpit supply in advance and not be left with an open date at the last minute. I also am careful to leave enough elbow room in the schedule so that there is flexibility for including some special event or message that cannot be anticipated. Usually I allow for about 10% flexibility, that is, one service in ten.

5. Now it is time to select the series of messages that will be included in the year. I enjoy preaching series of messages because they provide greater continuity and assure an accumulated impact. I have the information that has come from my conversations with the Elders and am ready to make my selections.

Each year usually has an extended series of messages from the Confessions of the Church that I include. So now I will chart out the sections of the confession that I anticipate I will be covering this year, mark those on the calendar and make note of the general content of each.

Usually six to eight other series are needed. Advent and Lent call for an appropriate series. The other series fit around those two major church seasons. The length of a series may vary from 3-10 messages. So I will block off the number of weeks required for each series and mark the title of the series on the calendar over those weeks.

6. Once the calendar has been charted out, I set up the resource file for each of those series of messages. These are my "incubators"! A special colored file folder is established for each one and clearly

labelled. The shelf behind me right now has incubators labelled "Sound Christians" (an expository study of II Timothy), "Doubters at Christmas", "Angels" (a short series prior to Advent), "Questions God Asks" (a winter series of messages), "Wonders At Calvary" (a Lenten series on miracles around the Cross), "Gems from Philippians 4", and then a summer series for next year, "Christians In The Valley" (a series of messages on suffering and how others have coped with it). I always keep these files visible and available because into them I expect to toss a wide variety of articles, cards, clippings, and scribbled notes over the next weeks and months. Periodically, I take an hour just to browse through each folder to stimulate my own imagination and search.

FLESHING IT OUT

I now have the potential for 75-80 sermons incubating all at the same time. I have a much clearer sense of direction for my pulpit ministry during the coming year. But at the appropriate time it must become more than a skeleton.

About a month ahead of the date on which a series is to begin more careful planning is necessary. The accumulated materials in the series file must be sorted. The series must be broken down to the number of intended messages, noting the passage and content of each one. At that time I set up a manila file folder for each individual sermon and divide the accumulated materials into the appropriate sermon file. Series files become sermon files in that way. Within each sermon file folder there will be a "Sermon Planning Sheet" (cf. Appendix B) on which I will note the pertinent information for this sermon, including the passage, purpose, and the major resources to be used. For the more lengthy Confessional series of messages I follow basically the same procedure and usually try to keep a few weeks ahead in doing the same.

Then by the 20th of each month I am ready to put together the worship and preaching schedule for the following month. The monthly schedule will include the sermon (with passage and title) for each service as well as any special events in the worship service that will influence the content of the service. The month is seen as a unit in that way.

Then I am ready to engage in more intensive research and exegesis for each message. I find that my study for each message goes so much more efficiently because of the long incubation process and the amount of material I have accumulated that relates to the passage. After research is completed, I can wrestle with how best to communicate that message to my congregation. Then I'm ready to write the manuscript.

I'm so much more comfortable with my preaching ministry when I always know where I'm going, when I'm never caught sermonless, and when I know that many sermons are incubating all the time.

SHARING IT

So far nearly everything has been done in the pastor's study. Outside of a congregational survey and some discussions in Elders' meetings, it all took place behind closed doors. On the one hand, that is appropriate because the final decisions about preaching selections and content belong to the preacher. On the other hand, the time must come when that information must be shared with others in order to cultivate their awareness of it and stretch them to an overall view.

I try to keep my Elders informed of my plans and progress, though the final decisions are mine. I also present the master calendar to the Worship Committee and Music Committee who are responsible for much of the planning of the worship services. It helps when they see the overall view as well as the specific events that need their attention. I also present the master calendar to the key musicians whose assistance I value so highly. Organists and Choir Directors have access to the master calendar so they can plan their season accordingly. Each monthly calendar which includes all the final information for each service is sent to the choir director, organists, key committee personnel, and the Children's Bulletin Editor. At times I also use the congregational newsletter to inform the congregation of what lies ahead.

If all this sounds like a lot of work, it is. The calling to preach is a calling to work, a lot of it. We must make no apologies for that. It is a task that is too strategic and significant to be handled lightly.

However, what wearies most preachers is not the amount of work that preaching requires, but how inefficient that work often becomes. This method of advanced planning, if followed carefully, will actually decrease the work-load of the pastor because it will enable him to become much more efficient. His reading program will be more directed. His accumulation of appropriate materials will be more successful. His sense of direction will be much clearer. He will feel better about it all! And so will his congregation!

So I challenge you to plan ahead. Be done with the frustration of wasted Mondays and Tuesdays wondering what to preach about. Be done with a misdirected and imbalanced preaching program because you haven't carefully planned it. Know where you are going! Be able to tell others where you are going! Enter a chapter in your ministry that will be more effective and more rewarding because it's carefully planned!

CONCLUSION

Mysteries will always surround the act of preaching. There will always be unanswerable questions about why a sermon reaches one person and not another. And in the final analysis we must confess that no real communication can take place unless the Spirit of God is present to fill the words of the preacher and touch the heart of the hearers.

But beware, preacher! It is far too easy to hide behind such mysteries and excuse our own insufficient efforts to perfect our skills. Preaching effectively is an art. And as with the practice of any art, it requires tireless efforts. A preacher who passionately thirsts for effectiveness will always be searching for those techniques and insights that will assure it.

Surely the Holy Spirit who opens the hearts of those who hear is the same Spirit who persistently prods the preacher on to greater diligence and growth. And undoubtedly the Spirit who grieves when some listen carelessly also grieves when others preach carelessly.

Our emphasis here is that the preacher who prays fervently for the power of God's Spirit to bless his homiletical efforts must also be the preacher who works hard at those very efforts. The Spirit of God becomes his motivator to work harder and not an excuse to work less.

There **are** practices and techniques that we can develop which will increase the effectiveness of our preaching.

The preacher who fails to carefully analyze his congregation cannot expect to be in touch with their world and their needs. Unless he studies them carefully he will not know how to adapt his method of presenting his message to them, and will not even be aware of this great deficiency! He may be an effective exegete, impressive crafter of words, and even an interesting orator, but without realizing it he may be presenting a message that would communicate well—but only with another audience! How sad when a potentially momentous act of preaching never really connects!

But how different, and how very satisfying, your preaching ministry will be when your elders participate with you in trying to carefully discern the needs of the members of your congregation and then your sermons are prepared and delivered with those people and their needs directly in view. That is the kind of preaching that connects! That is the kind of preaching that the Spirit uses best!

And when you carefully plan your preaching program in advance you will have ample opportunity to consider all the needs of your congregation. You will be delivered from Saturday night panic which tempts you to ignore their needs and put together whatever comes most easily. You will be delivered from the temptation to ride your own pet peeves and hobbies. Instead you will work with a broad overview of your preaching plans for the whole year and then you will be able to examine it for balance.

Those are the keys for a satisfying pulpit ministry—one that is in tune with the hearers, planned in advance and carefully balanced!

Situational Analysis Form

For Congregational Analysis in Preparation for Preaching

As someone who is very involved in the life of this congregation, you have received impressions and information that provides you with a knowledge of the personal needs of its members. There are many ways in which you may have received that knowledge—personal conversations, pastoral calling, family visitation, group interactions, etc.

You will provide vital assistance in the planning of preaching by indicating the matters that you believe preaching here must address during the coming year. Be sure that you make your selections below on the basis of what you believe *the congregation needs* and not just on what *your personal preferences* may be.

A. Questions of Faith – (please check the three most important ones)

_____ the assurance of salvation

_____ discerning God's will for our lives

_____ the need for personal conversion

_____ matters of eschatology (death, second coming, eternal state, etc.)

_____ stewardship (including finances, time, resources, creation)

_____ the life of worship

_____ witnessing and sharing our faith with others

_____ Christian education for children and youth

B. Matters of Doctrine – (Please check the three most important ones)

_____ salvation by the grace of God alone

_____ the person and work of Christ

_____ the nature and task of the Christian Church

_____ the work and power of the Holy Spirit

_____ sin and repentance

_____ the creation and providence of God

_____ the inspiration and authority of Scripture

_____ the greatness and sovereignty of God

C. Personal Growth – (Please check the three most important ones)

_____ preparing for and maintaining Christian marriages

_____ the responsibilities of Christian parenthood

_____ growing through affliction and suffering

_____ the dangers of an unforgiving spirit

_____ overcoming the tendency to be complacent

_____ overcoming fear and anxiety

_____ discovering and developing spiritual gifts

_____ establishing and maintaining better personal relationships

D. Moral/Ethical Issues – (Please check the three most important ones)

_____ abortion, euthanasia and issues of life

_____ alcohol, drugs and addiction

_____ materialism

_____ divorce and remarriage

_____ racism, prejudice and injustice

_____ poverty and world hunger

_____ world peace

_____ the relationship of church and state

E. Temptations – (Please check the three most important ones)

_____ greed, envy and jealousy toward others

_____ lust and adultery

_____ a critical spirit toward others

_____ a spirit of self-centeredness

_____ hedonism – the belief that life is for pleasure

_____ sabbath practices

_____ dishonesty and lying

_____ misplaced priorities

F. What other concerns do you have about needs that exist in the life of this congregation that you believe ought to be taken into consideration in designing a year of preaching that will be appropriate and relevant?

Thank you very much for your cooperation!

Sermon Planning Sheet

SERIES

    Name _____ No. in Series _____

    Theme _____

    _____

SERMON

    Title _____

    Text _____

    Central Theme _____

    _____

Introduction . . . .

Major Thoughts . . . .

Conclusion . . . .

Possible Hymns _____

www.ingramcontent.com/pod-product-compliance
Lightning Source LLC
Chambersburg PA
CBHW071058090426
42737CB00013B/2368